ARRANGING
The Basics of Contemporary Floral Design

BY HAL COOK, AIFD, AAF, PFC-I

With Arrangements by Surroundings

PHOTOGRAPHS BY BO PARKER

William Morrow and Company, Inc.
New York

A QUARTO BOOK

Copyright © 1985 by Quarto Marketing Ltd.

Library of Congress Catalog Card Number: 84-61862
ISBN: 0-688-02572-2

ARRANGING: The Basics of Contemporary Floral Design
was produced and prepared by Quarto Marketing Ltd.
15 West 26th Street
New York, N.Y. 10010

Editor: Karla Olson
Art Director/Designer: Richard Boddy
Illustrations: Susan Paradis

Typeset by BPE Graphics, Inc.
Color separations by Hong Kong Scanner Craft Company Ltd.
Printed and bound in Hong Kong by Leefung-Asco Printers Ltd.

Oasis®, Sahara®, and Iglu™ are the registered
trademarks of the Smithers-Oasis Company in Kent, Ohio.

2   3   4   5   6   7   8   9   10

Dedicated to the people of the floral industry
who have enriched my life through mutual teaching,
sharing, and encouragement.

CONTENTS

C O N T E N T S

CHAPTER 1

From Minimalism to High Construction

When you give flowers to someone, you are usually using them to convey a special message. The flowers express your feelings without a word being spoken—"I love you," "I care," "I'm sorry," "I'm happy," "I'm excited," or "Congratulations." Your thoughts and sentiments can take the form of a stunning single blossom or a dozen, a casual assortment or a tightly composed Victorian bouquet. Whatever the message, flowers can convey it eloquently.

But don't forget that flowers can also be bought for that very special someone—yourself. Whether to cheer you up after a long day or to enhance your home on a special occasion, flowers add color and a

Here is a straightforward, but extremely evocative arrangement. Three white lilies are arranged in a frosted vase to reflect the Ikebana placement of heaven, man, and earth. One bare branch is added to establish the correct proportion of one-third vase to two-thirds flowers. The flowers are so lovely themselves that they need no more accompaniment than the reaching branch, which emphasizes the celestial thrust of the highest lily.

breath of life to your surroundings. Let your imagination go; you'll find endless innovative ways to use them and numerous nooks and crannies where they will fit. A bouquet may be the perfect touch to complete your dining room decoration, or a single bloom may draw the eye to that unusual space in your living room. But no matter how you use them or where you place them, flowers should become an element of your interior decoration and your everyday life. They are yours to enjoy.

Thanks to excellent harvesting, preserving, and shipping facilities, fresh flowers are abundantly available in shops throughout the United States, Canada, the British Isles, and Europe. It is possible to stop in at your local florist's every day if you want, to pick up the perfect posy to add softness and personality to your home. Furthermore, flower arranging is no longer an intimidating skill attained after years of study—a prescribed art of carefully matched shapes, colors, and textures to produce a tightly constructed arrangement. The beauty of today's arrangements is in their freedom and inventiveness.

With this book you can easily learn the fundamental principles of floral design. After you've mastered these guidelines, you will see that you, too, can create fantastic and very individual arrangements for your own home, whether you choose two roses in a bud vase or twenty-five mixed blossoms in a basket. The key to the beauty and excitement of flowers is that your arrangement will be your very own, tailored perfectly to your home and your mood. And if you give flowers to

Certain occasions and settings call for a more complicated mass arrangement. Here, even though an amazing variety of flowers was used, each one has a distinct role in the overall design. The focal point, or center, is established by the striking form of the white and pink lilies and the intense colors of the zinnias. From this center, the arrangement thrusts outward in every direction, but a deliberateness of design defies confusion. The long strands of delphinium, dendrobium orchids, eucalyptus, and bare branches carry the eye out and beyond the reaches of the flowers. However, wherever the eye travels it meets a rose, strawflower, or lily that draws it back again to the focal point and the incredible unity of this bouquet. The result is that the viewer can contemplate this arrangement for a long time, without exhausting the possibilities of its astonishing beauty.

Here is a breathtaking example of how the sublime magnificence of a single blossom is allowed to shine in a minimal design. Who says a bouquet must include a number of flowers in a complicated pattern to be

beautiful? One bloom floating in a glass bowl is so simple and straightforward to assemble, and obviously so stunningly effective, that you have no excuse not to always have flowers throughout your home.

someone, the message they carry will be a personal and articulate one. With the inspiring range of colors, shapes, and textures that flowers have to offer, you are sure to enjoy the lovely, enlivening, beautiful world of flower arranging.

The Simple Beauty of Minimalism

For your own use around the home, minimal designs with one or two types of flowers are the simplest to put together and the most fun to set in various places. What could be a more cheerful sight than three vivid red carnations in a bud vase in the bathroom, to greet you just after you've woken up? Then a small arrangement of sunny yellow chrysanthemums or a bunch of assorted flowers from your own garden can decorate your breakfast table. A dozen gladioli loosely arranged in a tall vase can be placed on the porch for a special accent. Fragrant roses in assorted colors can be an exquisite centerpiece for your dining room table. Camellia blossoms floating in a shallow glass bowl will add romance to a candlelit dinner. All these suggestions require little effort or design talent. Even if you use very few flowers, their presence can be effective; it's up to you and your personal taste.

The Deliberate Creativity of Ikebana

Many of our ideas about flower arranging have been influenced by the Oriental tradition known as Ikebana, a highly structured art that is infused with symbolism. The most familiar type of Ikebana is arranged to reflect the natural world—earth, man, heaven—in specific places within the design. Ikebana requires a great deal of thought and planning

Contemporary designers today often celebrate the important influence of Ikebana by taking it a step further. In this arrangement, the "heaven-man-earth" theme of Japanese design is stated by the three deeply colored nerine lilies placed in a shallow bowl. Then the theme is echoed again with the lighter lavender freesia, and finally, implied by the downward sweep of the cymbidium orchids. The three prayer leaves fill out the arrangement, and with the pebbles in the dish, suggest the importance and grace of a natural setting.

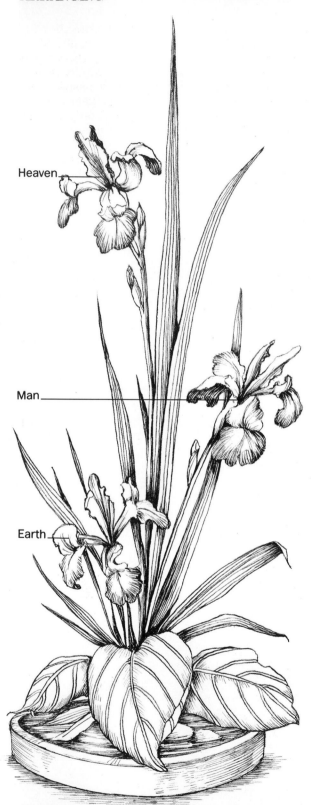

Heaven

Man

Earth

Orchids in Ikebana design of Heaven, Man, and Earth.

(as the many books on the subject will attest), and a Japanese hostess may take an hour or two to prepare one deceptively simple arrangement. Just a few flowers are used, and foliage, branches, and other natural elements such as stones, driftwood, and moss are often incorporated.

You do not need to train in Ikebana to appreciate its beauty or to incorporate its elegance and simplicity in your own designs. And, like all kinds of flower arranging, it is a great relaxer, a relief from the pressures of everyday life (no doubt lowering the blood pressure as you work), and allows you to use your own creativity, with a rewarding sense of accomplishment as a result.

Creating a Focal Point with Larger Arrangements

There is no doubt that the use of flowers in minimal arrangements is becoming increasingly popular in the United States and Canada because of influence from abroad—from Europe, where people buy flowers almost every day, as regularly as they do a loaf of bread. "Flowers are to nourish the soul, the bread to nourish the body."

Just as popular today are more complex arrangements for the home, often for special occasions. These are made by mixing several kinds of flowers and foliage in a larger display—for a centerpiece on the dining-room table, a color accent in a corner of the living room, to highlight a painting, or to enliven any spot where people congregate. They are a little more challenging to create, but not as difficult as they look. A wide range of arrangements fall into this category, and they are highlighted in this book, so you can see how your own creations can provide the perfect finishing touch.

The Glamour of High Construction

High construction, a new and different aspect of floral design which incorporates a greater number of flowers into a larger, more complicated arrangement, is just the opposite of minimalism. It requires more skill and experience and, naturally, uses more flowers. To decorate a hotel lobby, ballroom, conference room, or any other challenging location requires planning and careful consideration. The size of the room where the arrangement will appear, the colors in that room, the height of the ceiling, the placement of the furniture, the occasion for which the arrangement will be used, and the number of people who will occupy the room—all must be considered.

Master Florists of Holland

I once attended the preparation of a ballroom in New York City where a reception for Queen Beatrice of the Netherlands was to take place. Several designers from Holland transformed the hall into a wonderful flowerland of color and beauty. Masses of eight to ten foot displays adorned the walls with hundreds of blossoms in each arrangement. It was obvious that Dutch designers are true artists. They are required to go to arranging school for six or seven years before they are considered Master Florists and are eligible to open a flower shop. They are thoroughly trained in the growing, cultivation, care, and handling of flowers, and they assist other masters in design for several years before they graduate. They are specifically trained in exhibition work—a true art and a skill requiring a great deal of study. Today in America we are learning an immense amount from these master perfectionists. When it comes to high construction design, their expertise is inspiring to florists around the world.

This is territory for professionals, and we won't be focusing on high construction in this book. If you would like to acquire this skill, the best training is to be found either by working for a professional florist or by taking courses at one of the many design schools (see Sources, page 169).

CREATE AN EASY, BUT VERY PERSONAL, MINIMAL DESIGN FOR A SPECIAL PERSON OR TO CELEBRATE A NOTABLE DAY BY SIMPLY GATHERING A BOUQUET OF HIS OR HER BIRTH FLOWER OR THE FLOWER OF THE MONTH

MONTH	BIRTH FLOWER	FLOWER OF THE MONTH
January	Carnations	Carnations
February	Primroses	Violets
March	Violets	Jonquils
April	Daisies	Sweetpeas
May	Lilies of the Valley	Lilies of the Valley
June	Roses	Roses
July	Sweetpeas	Larkspur
August	Gladiolus	Gladiolus
September	Asters	Asters
October	Dahlias	Calendulas
November	Chrysanthemums	Chrysanthemums
December	Pointsettias	Narcissus

CHAPTER 2

Keeping Flowers Fresh

*B*uying the freshest flowers possible is essential, but it is only one part of the secret to the longevity of a floral arrangement. Although you will be anxious to use the flowers you've selected at the florist's or gathered in your garden, you'll need to have the patience to precondition them before you begin. This means delaying the actual designing for an hour or more, but preconditioning is the most important step to a beautiful and longer-lasting arrangement.

Try to get fresh-cut flowers so you can enjoy them longer. This is much easier than it might seem, even if you're nowhere near a garden. Today the flowers at your florist's may have traveled thousands of miles—from Holland, Israel, Italy, South Africa, Singapore, Hawaii, Colombia, or from Florida and California. All over the world, various types of flowers are harvested, then sorted, conditioned, packed, and air-freighted to the market where they will be sold. Air-freight service today is excellent, and flowers are usually given priority because of their fragility. Remarkably, they are usually available to the consumer twenty-four to forty-eight hours after they have been cut. This is why you can have almost any flower you desire, at any time of the year. Of course, locally grown flowers are available just a few hours after they have been cut, and home-grown blossoms are at hand any time you want them.

There are many signs to look for to make sure the flowers you select are fresh. Are the leaves green and firm, or are they beginning to wilt, brown, or yellow? These conditions tell you that the flowers were cut a few days ago and have probably been in cold storage for too long or were damaged by delays in shipping. Are the petals of the flowers also firm, and are their colors strong? Beware of bruises and folds in the petals. White spots on the petals are a sign of prolonged refrigeration with high humidity and poor air circulation (the flowers were packed too tightly and for too long). If the petals are discolored, the flowers are too old.

Once you have selected the flowers for your arrangement—and be sure to include some buds that will open later and keep your

Including a few buds amidst your fresh flowers, and removing all the leaves from at least the bottom of the stems, will certainly assure your arrangement the longest life possible. Here, two galax leaves appropriately cover the joint between flowers and vase, still allowing each individual bloom the space to shine in its own beauty.

arrangement looking fresh for longer—you must precondition them. A cut flower has been separated from its food- and water-seeking roots, so your aim is to simulate the work of the roots. The stem of a flower contains tubes called fibrovascular bundles, which transport nourishment from the roots up the stem to the flower. When a stem is cut and left out of water, nature starts to heal the cut by sealing it and closing off the tubes. Without water, the stem relaxes and the flower will wilt.

It is possible, however, to prevent the healing process and to allow the stem to continue to function. Place your flowers in about six inches of clean water at room temperature or warmer, and cut an inch or two off the end of the stems while they are under water. This ensures that water, not air, goes up the stem immediately. The stems should be cut with a clean, sharp knife or shears at a forty-five-degree angle (see drawing opposite). If the knife or shears are not sharp, the tubes may be squeezed together when the stem is cut, inhibiting the flow of water up the stem. And if the cut is made at a ninety-degree angle, the cut end of the stem may rest flat against the bottom of the vase, blocking its access to water and clogging it with sediment. Leave the flowers in the clean, fresh water for thirty minutes to one hour. If they do not seem to be responding by opening up or reviving, try cutting them under water again, one inch higher. You will cut into softer tissue, which will respond. As before, leave them in water for thirty minutes to one hour, then proceed with the preconditioning process.

When you cut the stems of the flowers, also remove any leaves from the part of the stem that will be under water. Water drawn up into the conducting tubes will escape through the leaves and never reach the blossom. The leaves left in the stagnant water will also cause a buildup of bacteria, result-

Only the stems of this lovely bouquet stand in water, and the mechanics of the arrangement, visible through the glass vase, actually enhance the design. The leaves have been removed from the lower half of the stems to ensure that water and important nutrients can flow directly to the flowers. A preservative added to the water has helped to intensify the brightness of the pink lilies and roses and the blue delphinium.

ing in an unpleasant odor. And above all, a clutter of leaves visible in the water will be messy and distracting.

Several types of flowers need special treatment at this stage. Daffodils, for instance, produce a milky substance when their stems are cut. This is like bleeding, and it expends nutrients and energy that the flower needs to live. In addition, the milky substance that runs from their stems, if allowed to leak into the water in which other flowers are arranged, will clog the tubes of the other flowers and choke them. So, after cutting the daffodil stems, let them stand out of water—dry—for half an hour, until they have stopped "bleeding." Then place them in fresh, warm water by themselves for an hour, to wash away any residue of the milky substance. Do not recut the stems, or the "bleeding" will start again. After these precautions, daffodils will be a bright and welcome addition to any arrangement.

If you select roses from your florist, the thorns will probably have been removed. However, if your roses are from your own garden, you will want to take off or blunt the thorns so you can handle them more easily. This should be done when you cut the stems so the wounds where the thorns were removed can also be soothed in the warm, fresh water. The key to thorn removal is gentleness. Florists now have machines that knock off the spikes with rubber mallets. At home, you will want to break each thorn off individually, sliding a sharp knife against the base of the spike. Do not slice down from above or you will tear the green bark of the stem. Each thorn should be removed with as clean and isolated a cut as possible, for too much scar tissue will build up around a large wound, clogging the conducting tubes. Or you can just cut off the pointy tips of the thorns with a sharp knife. After you remove or blunt the thorns, roses can be preconditioned with the rest of your floral selections.

Branches of imported dendrobium and oncidium orchids, and anthurium may seem somewhat worse for wear when they arrive from their overseas voyage. However, it is easy to revive them. Submerge the whole branch—flowers and stem—by laying it horizontally in a pan of water. Leave it in the bath for at least twenty minutes, then condition it as described below.

Because the lovely spring flower, amaryl-lis, has a hollow stem, it is quite a task for the flower to draw enough water up the stem to nourish it and create enough pressure to support the large blossom. So, turn the flower upside down and fill the stem with water. Then, place your thumb over the bottom to hold the water in the stem, and put it in a vase filled with conditioned water.

As in any science, new discoveries in floral care are being made all the time. For example, several years ago it was general practice to mash the woody stems of flowers such as the lilac. However, it has recently been determined that this wounds the stems, making it difficult for the blooms to receive nourishment. Now, a stronger chemical just for sustaining lilacs has been developed, which prevents bacteria, adds food, and adjusts the chemistry of the water to flow more easily up the stem. It is added to the conditioning water. In any case, after you've selected the flowers for your arrangements, be sure to ask your florist for any special instructions or procedures to keep them beautiful for as long as possible.

The next step is to provide food for the flowers. Transfer the flowers to the vase you are going to use, and fill it halfway with warm water. If you bought your flowers from a florist, he may have included a small package of preservative, which you should add to the water now. If they've come from your garden, you can make your own: Add one or two drops of chlorine bleach to the water (this kills any bacteria and helps keep the tubes open). Next, add a pinch of sugar. Sugar provides glucose, the food the flower needs to continue to develop in size and color. Place the container with the flowers in a cool spot and let the flowers absorb the food for another hour. Arrange them in conditioned water, but don't add more food, just fresh water, throughout the time you enjoy them.

Preconditioning your flowers is vital. It may seem to take a long time, especially when you're eager to begin arranging, but don't skip any part of this process if you want to ensure the flowers' longevity.

The single open rose and the three lilies here grab the viewer's attention, and all the other blossoms burst in radiating lines from this focal point. In this design, which requires the roses to be positioned very tightly together and some of the stems to be exposed, knocking off the thorns is very important.

CHAPTER 3

Colors at Work

Color is one of the most amazing—and unappreciated—factors of life. Try, for a moment, to imagine a world without color, in only black, white, and gray. There would be no sunny blue skies—every day would seem dreary and overcast. People would lose their individuality when stripped of their personal coloring. They would no longer have the power to enhance and manipulate their appearance with color in their clothes and makeup. The rooms in a house or apartment would blend together without separate, mood-setting decorative themes—the hominess of a red and blue country kitchen, or the warm, welcoming sophistication of a coral and cream living room. To everything, color adds excitement and diversity, depth and distinctiveness.

Plants and flowers are evidence of the remarkable power of color because the variety and intensity of their hues are completely natural and superbly eloquent. The bright, cheering yellow of the daffodil, the romantic red of a rose, and the soothing blue of an iris are just a few examples of the spectacular impact color can have on people and their moods.

Color, especially with flowers, should be very carefully used as a subtle tool to increase the beauty in life. But to use it effectively you must understand just how your perception of color comes about. Color may be defined as the reflection of light from a pigmented surface transmitted to the brain by the eyes. Colors cannot be touched, tasted, or smelled as "blue" or "yellow." We must be able to *see* color to appreciate it. Everyone reacts differently to various hues. Some colors make you happy; others may be depressing. We each gravitate toward certain colors, and usually our favorites remain the same throughout our lifetime.

Variations on Three Basic Colors

Knowing a few of the basic color principles may help you to observe the effects of color. There are three primary colors responsible for all other colors: red, yellow, and blue. The sources for primary colors must be found on earth in their natural state—they can't be created. Then we have the secondary colors, which are made by mixing the primaries. Red mixed with yellow produces orange, red and blue creates violet, blue and yellow gives us green. These six colors make up the base

In a typical Flemish arrangement, natural objects— such as fruit—are casually mixed with beautiful flowers, and colors are massed to emphasize their natural brilliance. Here, the pink rubrum lily, 'Journey's End,' establishes the height of the arrangement. The three remaining lilies then step down to complete the basic form of the arrangement. The blue irises are a very effective contrast to the pink tones. The bicolored tulips, massed low in the arrangement with the very fragrant white freesia and the peach-colored ixia, establish a pleasing focal point. Finally, the ivy softens the lines of the design, and the grapes add interest and color—deemphasizing the crystal vase. The result is an enhanced loveliness of the natural colors of each of the flowers.

The bold use of strong primary colors is in vogue today. Here, the triadic color scheme of red, blue, and yellow is very dramatic and contemporary. This bouquet is artfully designed with anemones, freesia, zinnias, bachelor's buttons, and Queen Anne's lace.

Yellow, green, blue, and violet—a pleasant analogous color combination for a bridal party. The assortment of flowers and colors here increases the interest and originality of the bouquet, with the additional bonus of a lovely, fresh fragrance.

The unexpected mix of pastels with bright yellow generates excitement in this arrangement. The yellow tulips and irises radiate from a common focal point like the sun's rays. The orange ixia, white bouvardia,

and pink alstroemeria and rambling roses add softness to the blend of flowers and colors. The hint of lavender from the delicate thistles fills out the exhilarating color spectrum.

of the color wheel. If a further division is wanted, we can mix a primary with a secondary color and produce an intermediate color. For example, by mixing orange, a secondary color, and yellow, a primary color, we produce a yellow-orange. Mix secondary color green with primary color blue, and we will get a blue-green hue.

We are creating strong, vivid colors, or hues. Adding white creates a tint, or lightening, of a color. Adding black gives us the shade, or darkening, of a color. If we add gray, we'll get a tone. For example, pink is a tint of red; burgundy is a shade of red; dusty rose is a tone of red.

How Colors Work Together

To enjoy color beyond the monochromatic—a single hue with its tints, shades, and tone—you may turn to the harmony of complementary colors. These are the colors directly opposite one another on the color wheel: red and green, orange and blue, yellow and violet. Complementary colors are essential in flower arranging because they go well together, especially when we combine several tints and shades of complementary colors in an arrangement.

Another useful combination for flower arranging is triadic color. Triadic colors are those that are equidistant from one another on the color wheel. Blue, red, and yellow are triadic, as are orange, green, and violet. Then there is the analogous color combination, which is very pleasing to the eye and is the most commonly used in arranging flowers as well as in interior decorating. This is the combination of any three or four colors touching one another on the color wheel. Red, orange, yellow is a warm, exciting analogous color combination. (Add green if you want a fourth color.) Blue, violet, and red is a royal analogous color combination; and green, blue, and violet work together as a cool analogous combination.

But even these basic, primary colors in

The royal colors of agapanthus, liatris, and delphinium are enriched by the addition of extra-deep-purple lycanthus. This is a magnificent background for a stunning array of orchids and lilies. The informal basket container fades underneath this beautiful analogous color scheme, focusing all attention on the glorious flowers.

Simplicity is understated elegance and, due to this minimalism, color becomes especially important. Here, three bright pink nerine lilies, representing heaven, earth, and man, set the line for this ikebana-inspired arrangement. The four darker allium add another dimension of height and a new depth to the form. The two light pink cymbidium orchids balance the arrangement by bringing weight to the base of the design, and they complete the spectrum of the soft colors. The loose, ribbony effect of the grass, the low white bowl, and the black stones all accentuate the oriental influences in this contemporary design.

In this grouping of analogous colors, tints and shades of red, blue, and purple are blended to create a rich visual design. The fascinating and diverse mixture of floral types is unified by the central color scheme, and finally joined by the use of similar vases. It is a fresh, unique, and charming idea to have three independently lovely arrangements complement one another when placed together. Grouping them together on a mirrored table adds depth and sparkle to their visual effect. Enjoy them like this for a day or two, then scatter them around the house to echo their loveliness throughout.

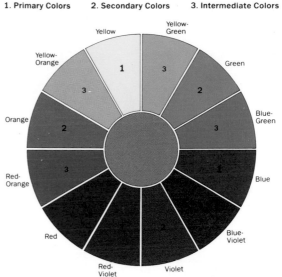

1. Primary Colors   2. Secondary Colors   3. Intermediate Colors

their various combinations could become boring if they were used in only one intensity. Therefore we add variation by using the tints and shades of a color.

Using Color in Flowers

Understanding color and its use can be tremendously helpful when selecting your flowers. Strong, pure colors create a strong statement. Pastel colors make a more subtle statement. When you are designing an arrangement with a particular person in mind, consider his or her personality when you choose the colors.

The proportions of color are also important in a flower arrangement. When dealing with three colors, as in analogous color combinations, it is better to use more of the lighter color and less of the darker. The suggested proportion is sixty-five percent of the lightest color, twenty-five percent of the middle color, and ten percent of the darkest available. Darker colors also look best around the focal point of the arrangement.

There is so much to learn and appreciate about color that entire books have been written on the subject. Experiment on your own for the combinations you like best.

Here is an example of the warm analogous color scheme of red, orange, and yellow, enriched with a tint of pink. The brightness of the sun that helped these flowers grow is embodied in this cheerful arrangement.

CHAPTER 4

The Elements and Principles of Design

When creating your flower arrangement you must consider certain elements and principles of design in order to produce a visually pleasing and unified composition.

The five elements of design—the "tools" you work with in arranging—are form, space, line, texture, and color.

Form is the overall shape of the arrangement. It includes the height, the width, and also the depth. We will discuss the various basic forms of arrangements more extensively later in this chapter.

Space is the emptiness left around each flower. Space is needed to enhance each individual leaf, blossom, or branch, giving it importance and allowing the viewer to enjoy the parts that make up the whole. A bunch of flowers all touching creates a mass of color, but it does not allow for an appreciation of each flower in the arrangement.

Line is the outline of your arrangement—whether it is triangular, round, oval, or an open curve. It also includes accent lines

This tall centerpiece, with a country theme, is a traditional gathering of wildflowers. The dominance of white and yellow immediately captures the eye. Then the continuous rhythm of the arrangement carries the eye from the two orange tiger lilies, with their contrasting form, around the bouquet—with the surprising bursts of lavender from the ageratum, upward with the height of the three cattails, and back down by the balance of color in the earthy terra cotta container. Natural looking, but actually very deliberate, this is a solidly balanced design.

within the outline, such as radiating lines or lines crossing through the arrangement. For more on line, see Chapter 9, "Line Arrangements: Flowers and Branches," page 100.

Texture applies to the tactile quality of the container, flowers, foliage, and accessories. The best effect is achieved when similar textures are combined. Silky red roses are better displayed in crystal than in terra cotta, and marigolds and zinnias would look better in terra cotta than in crystal.

Color selection is responsible for a design looking great—or being hopelessly dull. The proper colors can command attention, receive the greatest praise, and warm the coolest heart. Color excites, it inspires, it emphasizes, and it persuades.

Equally important are the principles of design—those qualities that please the eye of the viewer. The principles to keep in mind and strive for when creating your arrangements include unity, scale, accent, balance, harmony, and rhythm.

Unity is the feeling of oneness—that all the parts, including vase, foliage, flowers, and colors, belong in this arrangement.

In working toward unity in an arrangement, it is important to recognize the "class distinctions" between flowers and to choose accessories accordingly. Orchids and roses are in a class of their own; they are "quality," and they deserve the best when you select a vase, foliage, or even when you wrap them for delivery: velvet or satin ribbons suit orchids and roses better than burlap or plaid. Carnations, gerbera daisies, irises, and the dozens of other greenhouse-grown flowers are in another class, and, therefore, less extravagant accessories should be used. Many of the garden flowers, like geraniums, pansies, petunias, ageratum, zinnias, and marigolds, would look lovely in plastic or wooden containers, or in unusual homemade containers. Because these are garden flowers, earthy accessories are appropriate, such as branches, pine cones, or a burlap ribbon. In

A rainbow of flowers, in full harmony, is arranged loosely in a clear bubble bowl to give the round form of this arrangement a modern, natural look. The foliage is kept above the water level on some of the floral stems to fill out the design naturally. The unity of this arrangement is so complete that not one flower needs to be added or taken away.

any case, make sure all parts of the arrangement are suited to one another and become a unified whole.

Scale is a matter of size and its relationship to each part of the arrangement. The smaller the flowers, the smaller the vase should be. A pansy in a six-inch vase is lost and out of scale. A long-stemmed rose in a four-inch vase is also inappropriate (as well as top-heavy). A mixture of lilies of the valley with Easter lilies is an example of flowers out of scale with each other. Scale is discussed in greater detail in Chapter 11, "Miniatures," page 122.

Accent is best created with the color or size of a flower, often at the focal point of the design. The focal point is the center of attention in a design, or the point from which the design originates. To place one orchid at the focal point of an arrangement would be to create an accent. The orchid would be the most prominent and dominating single flower. To add five red roses to an all-white arrangement would be to accent the roses within a mass of white. If you want to emphasize something to draw attention to one area, or to stress a point in your arrangement, you would do it with an accent.

Balance is correct when the arrangement looks sturdy enough to stand on its own and not topple over at the slightest movement. A well-balanced design—and one that's easy to visualize—is a triangle with the highest flower centered over the vase and placed deeply enough in the vase to ensure a stable position. All the other flowers are below that top one, in front or to the side. Keeping the lighter flowers on the outer part of the arrangement and the darker colors toward the center will also give a heavier appearance to the base, which is pleasing to the visual balance of the arrangement.

Harmony is the effective matching and blending of materials. For example, including a variety of flowers that break the monotony and yet work together to achieve a delib-

Here is a group of truly harmonious materials. The reaching branches establish the correct proportion to balance the round glass bowl container, and they add dramatic height. Alstroemeria and orange lilies offer special and interesting shapes to a casual garden theme. Goldenrod, freesia, and brodieae fill out the open round form and enhance the refreshing "just picked" look.

erate effect is one way to harmonize your arrangement. Use a few spike flowers, like liatris or larkspur, along with a few round flowers, like carnations or chrysanthemums. Add a few feathery celosia and a branch of lilies and you develop a harmony of flowers. And by selecting your colors equally carefully, you will have harmony of color—those that blend and belong together.

Rhythm allows the viewer's eye to take a quick trip through the arrangement. You see each flower and enjoy the differences, appreciating the blending of colors and the movement of the foliage, twigs, and branches within the arrangement. Rhythm also draws the eye to the focal point.

Most of these elements and principles are incorporated in all good designing. However, at times color will be more pronounced than texture; at other times you may emphasize space, as in a contemporary design, with less attention to accent; or you may be concerned with color harmony rather than scale. Although you may want to emphasize one or two elements or principles more than you do the rest, you must never overlook any of them.

Form in Design

The first question you will deal with when you are applying these principles to your design will have to do with form. What shape, or form, will the arrangement take, within which all these other factors will play a role?

Floral design is based on three-dimensional geometric forms.

Lines
Triangles (pyramids, cones)
Curves
Circles (spheres)
Angles

Symmetrical triangle: This is a useful basic design because it is well balanced. It is a very popular form and an easy one to construct. It allows for the use of many flowers of assorted colors and all kinds of assorted accessories—which is why it is the basis of most Victorian designs.

Asymmetrical triangle: This form is particularly effective when it is used to feature, draw attention to, or accent a center attraction. For example, left and right asymmetrical triangles on either side of a statue, a

FORMS AND HOW THEY ARE USED

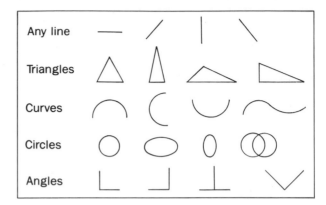

Any line				
Triangles				
Curves				
Circles				
Angles				

Symmetrical triangle

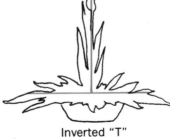

Asymmetrical triangle

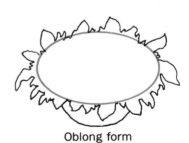

Combination of two triangles

Line form: a corsage

Inverted "T"

Oblong form

Round form

Formal round
centerpiece—Continental

Informal round
centerpiece—Contemporary

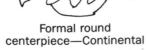

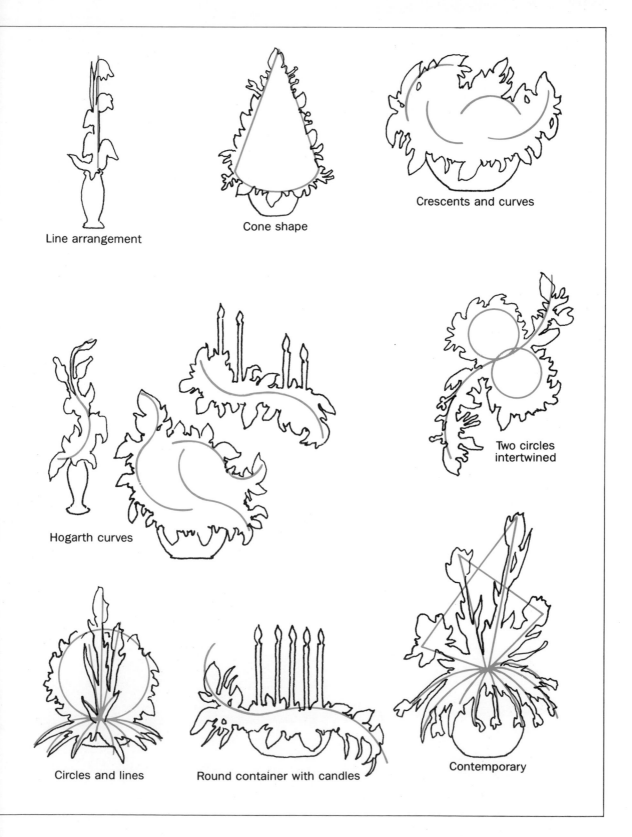

Line arrangement

Cone shape

Crescents and curves

Hogarth curves

Two circles intertwined

Circles and lines

Round container with candles

Contemporary

Form, harmony, and unity have all been carefully considered in this pleasing and beautiful oblong centerpiece. Its dimensions are perfect for the center of a dining table—low enough to be seen over and reaching to the ends of the table. Harmony and unity are established by the softness of both the flowers

and their pastel colors—the white lilies, the lavender freesia and alstroemeria, and the pink rambling roses. Finally, the Queen Anne's lace fills out the design, and would echo a white lace tablecloth and soft candlelight, the perfect background for the lovely centerpiece.

mirror, a painting. It's a smartly styled look, very elegant when the arrangements are tall and sweeping.

Combination of two triangles: This form is often used on a mantelpiece, a banquet table, or in a sympathy arrangement. The widest part of the design—where the two triangles meet—is the focal point, with the forms ascending and descending from this center. This could also be considered a diamond shape, when the ascending and descending triangles are the same size.

Line arrangements: These are great for an Oriental look, or for the looser, simpler contemporary style. They are particularly effective when displayed in a setting where space is limited.

Angle form: The term "angle" is used extensively in floral design, but when referring to the form of an arrangement it has a more definitive meaning. Specifically, an angle design is a scalene—or asymmetrical—triangle: all three sides are of different lengths. Within those perimeters, there are many, many sizes and shapes that can be used. The angle form is one of the most versatile, and it is very useful for arrangements that are designed to accent a separate object, such as a statue, or a point in a room.

Inverted "T": This form is actually a variation of an angle design. It is very much in vogue today because it can be stylish without requiring a great number of flowers. It is a dramatic, high-style design.

Oblong form: This is a useful design for rectangular tables. Oblong centerpieces look best when they measure about one-quarter the length of the table.

Round form: Mostly used for centerpieces, this shape has a continental look when designed with a variety of flowers and colors. The circumference of the arrangement can be adjusted according to the size of the table on which it appears and the number of guests who will be seated there.

A round form with a smoothly curved top, like a dome, is a more formal, traditional, continental look. Keep the arrangement airy, less molded looking, if you are entertaining informally. A contemporary round arrangement will have more variation in its contour.

Cone shape: This is a symmetrical triangle in a round container, which can be very pleasing. Open space throughout the arrangement makes the individual flowers stand out prominently. Crowding the flowers together creates a color impact, but is not a good design. The flowers need to breathe.

Crescents and curves: There are dozens of uses of crescents and curves, and every designer tries to create an original arrangement with these forms. The curve can form any number of shapes: an arc sweeping downward, a "C" flowing up to the sky, or an evenly hanging curve like a scale.

Two curves flowing into each other to form an open "S" shape make up what is called a Hogarth curve. This design has good rhythm and is pleasing for an upright arrangement or for a flat centerpiece on a buffet table. It can be exciting and dramatic or can be classic, as when two curves are used on a dining table; an arrangement in a Hogarth curve is bound to elicit compliments and admiration when tall candles are placed within the curves.

Two circles intertwined represent friendship or love. A Hogarth curve running between them creates rhythm, accent, and with the proper use of color, an added element of harmony.

Combining circles and lines will create another dramatic look. Try a wreath of yellow flowers combined with curves of orange and lines of red. Add some green foliage to your analogous color arrangement and you'll have a smart, classic, and dramatic design.

A round container with tall vertical burgundy candles, curves of pink carnations, and assorted green foliage will add intrigue and romance to any evening.

It's always interesting to examine a design that is very contemporary. You'll see that it's made up of the familiar triangles, angles, circles, and lines. Anything is possible when the basic forms are used. Try one of these suggestions, or create your own combination of forms, and you will see the effect flowers can have. Be daring and creative.

This arrangement is an outstanding example of the importance of space, line, and form. With striking simplicity, it shows how every element of design should be carefully considered. The space given to each lovely lily emphasizes its individual importance and beauty. The basic triangle form and the upward thrust of the vertical lines of the branches add a pleasing balance using a minimum number of flowers.

CHAPTER 5

Containers

The selection of a container can either add to or detract from all of your artistic efforts. Actually, it is often the container that gives you the clue and inspiration for the arrangement. A French country bouquet would certainly be out of place in a shiny black contemporary vase, and would be much more appropriate in a moss-lined basket. The modern vase calls for a high-style arrangement of a few flowers, vivid in color, with open space and strong lines.

The union between container and arrangement embodies many of the elements found in a good marriage—unity, balance, and harmony. The elements must work together to form one beautiful, cohesive unit—neither one overpowering the other. Your container not only performs a vital function in an arrangement, by providing the receptacle in which the design will be placed, but it must also be an esthetically pleasing part of the design as a whole.

Choosing a container for a particular design is as critical as choosing the flowers to be placed in it, if the overall effect is to be successful. Nowhere is this more evident than when the designer is choosing the container and flowers for a minimal contemporary arrangement or an Oriental design. Because fewer flowers are used, the container itself becomes more significant and noticeable, and has more impact on the overall design. Shape, color, and texture are all introduced—and at this point the container becomes a co-star with the flowers, not just a supporting actor.

It is ideal to have a variety of containers on hand. Glass, plastic, and pottery or ceramic containers are the best choices. You can find plastic containers today that are exact replicas of glass containers—just as beautiful and at a much lower cost. They also come in a breathtakingly wide variety of colors, shapes, and sizes.

Glass, pottery, and ceramic are also easier to clean than metal, which has a rough inner surface. Preservatives are apt to cause pitting in metal. If you want to use your silver or precious metal bowls, however, place a plastic bowl inside to hold the water, or line the metal bowl with tin foil. In any case, all containers should be cleaned with a solution of detergent and chlorine bleach after every use, to prevent the growth of bacteria.

The selection of a container depends on how it is to be used, the mood you want to create, and the setting in which it will ap-

When a primarily white Oriental arrangement is placed in a tall crystal vase it becomes quintessential elegance. The white amaryllis blossoms and fragrant tuberoses provide the necessary vertical lines for this container, and this heavenward thrust is emphasized by the bamboo. These branches could be extended even higher if your setting permits. The clusters of dendrobium orchids form radiating lines from the sides, which balance the lofty vertical lines, and the white quince branches unify the whole design. The ming fern camouflages the mechanics of the arrangement and, along with the stones scattered at the base of the vase, echoes the Oriental influence of the design.

CONTAINERS

Baskets

Terra cotta vases

Glass/crystal vases

Ceramic vases

Bud vases

Bowls

A low open bowl has so many uses. One exquisite blossom can be floated enchantingly in it, or a number of exotic flowers can be effectively displayed. In this arrangement, the flowers are the principal actors and the vase is in a supporting role. With a sturdy pinholder or "frog," the vase will securely hold four

pincushion protea, six anthurium, a number of blush dendrobium orchids, and several camouflaging caladium leaves. The openness of the container lets each element stand out on its own, but in perfect harmony with the other ingredients of the Ikebana-inspired design.

A black vase definitely enhances the brilliance of the flower it contains. Here, the vivid yellow of the freesia radiates from the sleek container, and you can almost see the flowers' springtime fragrance. The raffia bow adds a pleasing contrast in texture, in the same fascinating way the classic shape of the container opposes the casual "drop-in" style of the bouquet. The overall effect is strikingly beautiful, very contemporary, and very simple to put together yourself.

A grapevine basket is the perfect container for this American garden design. Overflowing with dark pink rambling roses, "Sterling Silver" roses, lavender freesia, white tulips, deep purple butterfly bush, and accents of Queen Anne's lace and hardy green ivy, this bouquet could be freshly picked. Baskets, filled with absorbent floral foam covered with moss, have recently become an important container for a variety of reasons: they come in numerous sizes and shapes, are inexpensive, and add an interesting texture to an arrangement.

pear. If your home is contemporary in style and furnishings you may need a few cylindrical containers, from 6 to 12 inches tall, in conservative colors—gray, black, or white. This works for an art deco look, or for a very subdued style. In this case the flowers are making the statement and the container functions as background. The cylinder shape allows plenty of room for long-stemmed flowers and supports heavy accent materials like curly willow branches, bamboo, cattails, grasses, and other natural accessories. It's great for dramatic lines and using space to accent your minimal use of flowers. In fact, if it's a casual look you want, cylinders are great for only six, nine, or a dozen loose, long-stemmed flowers. Add a few pieces of foliage, or none if you prefer, and in minutes you have a touch of color that tells your guests you cared enough and took the time to make their visit a memorable occasion.

Round bubble-type containers are also versatile for a loose arrangement of short-stemmed flowers—fashionable with a high-style contemporary look.

When shopping for your containers, consider a variety of colors, sizes, shapes, and even textures. I've seen milk bottles used too often in lieu of a vase. I've also seen a Coke bottle used as a bud vase for a teenage party, and it looked great for that occasion. Neither would look right for a formal arrangement, as that gift of "petal perfect" long-stemmed red roses certainly deserves a proper complement when you select a vase.

Bud vases, bowls, shallow dishes, usual and unusual vases of assorted colors and textures only encourage you to do your very best in creating floral arrangements that reveal your personality and individuality.

A sturdy glass block is an excellent and stable container for a one-sided design incorporating a number of breathtaking flowers. The oblong opening of the vase lets you spread the blossoms enough to give each one the space to be fully appreciated even if yours is not a minimal arrangement. Here, glass marbles are added to hold the stems in place, but they also give texture and importance to the beautiful block as an integral part of the floral design. The stems of the pink rambling roses, purple and white licianthus, pink wildflowers, and branches of heart-shaped ivy are visible, crisscrossing gracefully in a fascinating mesh, which further enhances the stunning beauty of the arrangement.

CHAPTER 6

The Mechanics of Arranging

One long-stemmed rose in a crystal bud vase requires no assistance to look elegant and beautiful. But many other types of arrangements do need the help of some "mechanics"—and in turn, some finishing touches to hide those mechanics. As with all art forms, we want to view and enjoy the finished product without being forced to see how the effect was accomplished. The necessary mechanics in floral designing include picks, wires, floral foams, tapes, and various types of holders to anchor the stems. But first, a word about the tools you need to have on hand for efficient flower arranging.

There are only a few essential tools you will want to have while you are designing. You must have a sharp knife. It should be a convenient, easy-to-handle size, with a blade not longer than six inches. A firm kitchen knife will do, or you may choose to purchase a special florist's knife.

You will also want two pairs of shears: one for cutting wires and stems and the other for cutting ribbon. Be sure to use each for only one purpose. They are worn down in different ways by their respective jobs, and shouldn't be abused. Finally, be sure to have several buckets of water available for holding the flowers during the preconditioning process, and for keeping the flowers you don't

This simple, casual arrangement of blush orchids, nerine lilies, and vivid caladium leaves is very secure in its tall, weighted vase. The clear marbles not only add interest, but they hold the stems in place and give reassurance that the whole arrangement will not topple over with the slightest bump.

use in one arrangement fresh for the next.

One of the basic and most useful devices for anchoring your flowers in a container, especially a shallow one, is a pinholder, sometimes called a "frog." This is a heavy metal base covered with pinpoints—like a one-dimensional hedgehog. The stems are anchored on the pinpoints, at any angle you want. Pinholders come in many shapes and sizes, from tiny round ones to larger rectangular shapes. You can also find them encased in a metal cup, to hold water, which is handy if you're planning to use a nonwaterproof container like a basket. Another holder, good for heavier flowers and long stems, also has a heavy metal base but with a lattice-like cage of heavy wire over it, which holds the stems in place a few inches above their tips. You can even find holders that are a combination: wire cage over a pinpoint base.

Other anchors are available too, and are useful for different types of containers. Clear or colored marbles are pretty in a crystal bowl and don't need to be hidden. (But if you do want to hide a holder in a glass bowl or vase, try using smooth black Oriental pebbles for a handsome effect.) And there are holders you can make yourself: In a tall opaque container, you can insert woody twigs, cut so they won't show, to fill up the space and prevent long-stemmed flowers from flopping over the rim.

Floral foam, the most popular of which is called "Oasis®," also acts as an anchor, holding the flowers in position. The foam is a firm, porous substance, one block of which can absorb up to two quarts of water from the container and supply it to the stems. If you add water to the container daily, the flowers will receive a constant supply, wherever they are placed in the foam.

Grouping three independent but harmonious vases together produces a very effective centerpiece with a contemporary flair. In this multi-level design, the viewer sees each individual arrangement, the unity of the three together and the continuation of the arrangement in the reflection in the mirror. The marbles in the vases and on the mirror add effervescence and draw the vases more closely together as a whole. Finally, note the carefully positioned caladium leaves that smooth the joint between flowers and vase. There seems to be no separation as they just flow together and continue intriguingly into the depths of the mirror.

AN ARRANGER'S TOOLS, SUPPLIES, AND PROCEDURES

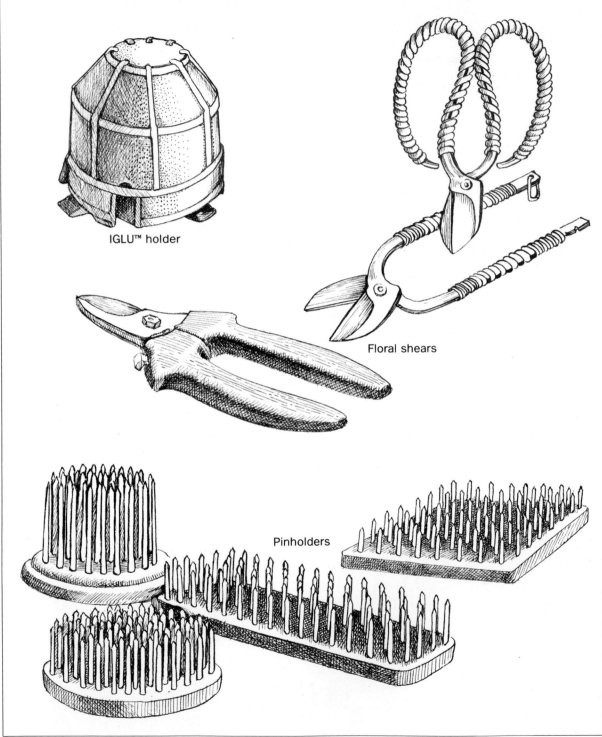

IGLU™ holder

Floral shears

Pinholders

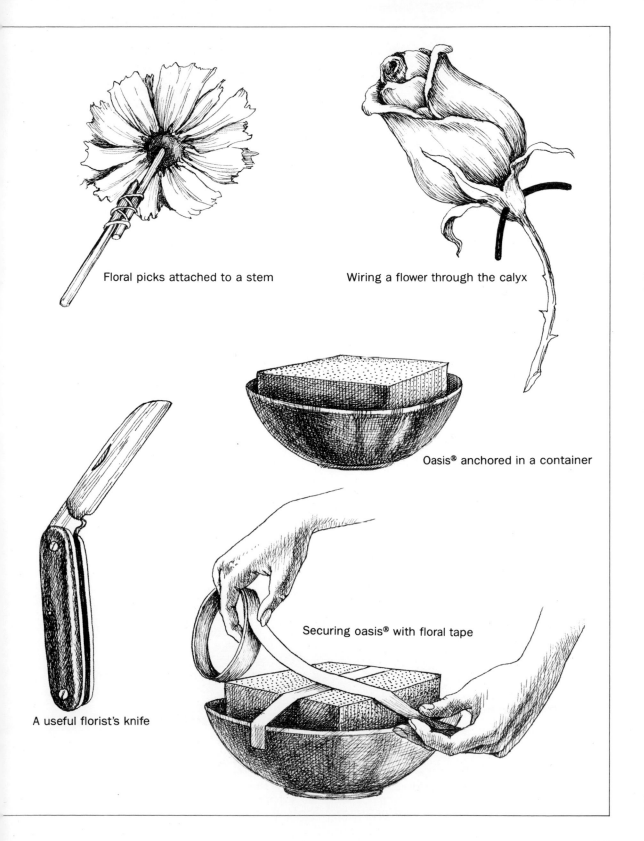

Floral picks attached to a stem

Wiring a flower through the calyx

Oasis® anchored in a container

Securing oasis® with floral tape

A useful florist's knife

No arrangement could be more simple to design and assemble than three perfect gardenias floating in open containers. Yet their elegance commands undivided attention. The variety of containers adds an interesting degree of contrast. The marbles, used to support the stems and leaf collars of the blossoms,

provide texture and unify the three bowls. Strategically, they also hide the messy mechanics, which otherwise might be reflected in the mirror. Instead the reflection doubles both the size and the effect of the arrangement, and creates the illusion that the blossoms are floating in a pond.

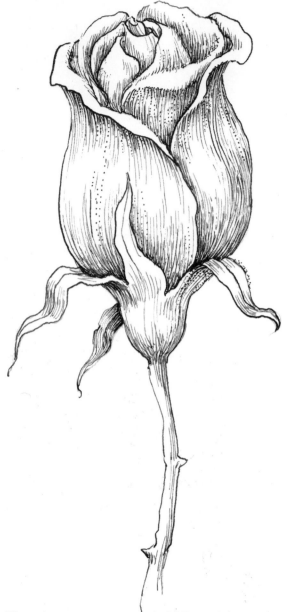

The calyx acts as a cup to hold the petals.

The green color of the foam also functions as camouflage. It can be further disguised by adding short pieces of foliage, or several three-inch leaves, such as galax leaves. In a shallow bowl, where the foam might still be visible, you can add more foliage or a flower or two deep into the arrangement to cover any empty spot—or moss, creating the effect of make-believe earth.

If the container is at least two or three inches deep, it will hold the foam securely.

You may have to cut the foam to fit the container, and you want it to fit snugly, but always allow some room around it for adding water. You may even cut a wedge or square section out of the foam, so you will have a reservoir where you can check the water level, and into which you can pour fresh water.

If you use a shallow dish, the foam could slide when the container is moved. To prevent this, plastic-coated waterproof tape is used to anchor it. Place the dampened foam in a dry container, and run a piece of tape over the foam, securing the ends to the edge of the container. You will probably need at least two pieces of tape to lock the foam in place. After you have arranged your flowers in the foam, you can use bits of foliage or other decoration to cover both the foam and the tape. Waterproof tape comes in green and white; use white on white containers and green for most others. A new clear tape has recently appeared on the market; it can be used on any container.

The "Iglu™" is a new and very useful flower holder. Basically, it is floral foam contained in a plastic cage which is dome-shaped like an Eskimo's igloo. It is especially versatile because, with its sturdy outer cage, it can be attached to almost anything—wreaths, branches, a chandelier, a newel post, a statue—almost anywhere you can imagine. If you soak the "Iglu™" in water for a few minutes, it will retain enough moisture to keep flowers fresh for several days.

Some flowers have weak stems, or have such large blossoms that the weight causes them to droop. This is where florist's wire is useful—it supports the flower and straightens out the stem, allowing it to continue to take up water. You can also use wire to bend the stems of your flowers into natural-looking graceful curves.

Florist's wire comes in different sizes and weights. The lower the gauge number, the heavier the wire. More delicate work requires a higher-number gauge, which is lighter in weight and more flexible. If you need a wire for a gladiolus, ask for #21–22 gauge, which is strong enough for its heavy stem. Carnations may require #22–23 gauge, or #24–26 gauge if you are doing some intricate work. A good all-around wire would be #22 gauge.

To use the wire, cut a piece as long as you would like your stem to be. Carefully insert it up from the bottom of the blossom head—called the calyx—through the center. Be sure you do not stick the wire so far into the flower that it can be seen from the top. Then wrap the wire around the calyx a couple of times, and run it straight down the stem.

Another way to wire your flowers is to cut a piece of wire twice as long as your stem and run it straight through the calyx from side to side. Pull the wire through until the bloom is in the middle, then bend it so both pieces of wire run down the stem and meet at the bottom. This method adds extra stability, durability, and support.

At times floral picks are used to extend the stem of a flower. They are usually three to six inches long and are attached to the base of the stem. Their pointed ends make them easy to stick into your floral foam.

Floral tape covers up the mechanics when you use florist's wire and picks. It comes in white, light green, dark green, black, brown, tan, pink, blue, orchid, red, yellow—just about any color you would need for flower/stem color coordination or for that decorator touch. Green is the most popular, since it is the color of most flower stems and looks natural when it is used. White is popular in wedding designing, and black might be used on a boutonniere for a dark suit. Floral tape comes in one-half-inch and one-inch widths; the narrower size is easier to handle.

To use the tape on a wired stem, start under the blossom. Wrap the tape around once or twice to secure it, and then stretch the tape out. Twist the stem into the stretched tape, keeping the tape pulled down along the stem. This will hide your mechanics with a thin covering, simulating a new stem. Wrap the tape firmly as you go, but don't squeeze the stem or cover the cut end. It should still be able to take up water.

When wiring birds, flowers, cones, foliage, or other accessories to branches in your arrangement—for instance, silk dogwood blossoms to branches for a decorative tree—you can use either hot glue (see your florist for help) or tape the flower or accessory to the branch with floral tape. If the branch is brown, use brown tape; if it is dried and tan, use tan tape; if you sprayed it black for a decorative look, then use the black tape. Make it look as natural, unobtrusive, and as neat as possible.

It is always much easier to work with wired flowers when creating a corsage. They are more stable because it is possible to bend and manipulate them so they can be positioned closely together. They should be gathered in a tight design so the corsage is more likely to remain intact if knocked or bumped off. And if they are wired, the heavy weight of the stems is eliminated so the corsage is more comfortable to wear. Use a wire of #22–23 gauge, which is less bulky than the natural stems but very sturdy. Remove the stems and attach the wires with tape as described. (Remember, when your work requires that you touch the blossoms, always keep your hands wet. The water will act as a protective coating so you won't bruise the petals.) Tape all the wires into position once they are bent together. Make sure there are enough layers of tape around the wires so you can pin the corsage through them into place on the shoulder or waist.

Today, many contemporary designs incorporate the mechanics of the arrangement into the intended visual effect. The stems weave in and out among each other, forming a natural holder that is visible through a clear glass vase, and creates an intriguing texture when magnified by water. This latticework is arranged as deliberately as the blossoms are.

Sometimes, grape vines or branches are used to form a framework for both the top and the mechanics of an arrangement. Their swirls or linear forms add unity to the design. The vines twist in and out of the container, among the stems and flowers; the branches thrust down into the vase as they reach high into the air above the container.

New products and ideas are constantly being introduced in the floral industry. They improve our speed, artistry, and versatility. However, they are almost all used as mechanics, to improve our designs and facilitate the work. So we must continue to invent ways of covering up the mechanics. Give your camouflage a natural look so it does not intrude, and you'll enjoy your design more and more. Spanish moss, introduced a few years ago, is good for disguising foam, as are ground moss, and even pine chips and deer moss. But don't forget the imaginative and effervescent ways you can use colored or clear marbles. No matter what you use, make sure that it ensures and enhances the unity of the arrangement.

CHAPTER 7

Contemporary Styles

"Contemporary" refers to the one style that is always changing: the style of today, of the times. It reflects current tastes in interiors, clothes, and other areas of design, whether a modern interpretation or a futuristic one. As people change, fashion trends change, and so will styles in flower arranging. They will echo the lifestyle of the moment, and the most successful and expressive contemporary styles will become established "classics" tomorrow.

Of course, each person's use of flowers and interpretation of current design trends will express that person's individuality. The more carefree the person, the more carefree the design—perhaps just a single blossom or a few, casually placed. Others will enjoy a simple design, a bit more crafted, with less than a dozen flowers. And others will want an artful profusion of flowers and colors.

This enjoyment of self-expression can be seen in the current boom in sales of loose flowers, rather than arrangements. Customers can be creative without necessarily incurring much expense. And florists, no longer required to spend as much time arranging, can concentrate on providing an exciting array to choose from.

As you will see in the illustrations, contemporary design, however individualistic, does have certain recognizable characteristics. The use of foliage is minimal. Instead, the focus is on the flower itself and on the space around it. Although most of these arrangements are not bound by the standards mentioned in Chapter 4, you will see definite lines—curves, angles, triangles, and other familiar forms—and, above all, balance. At first the designs may seem Oriental in appearance, but they go beyond the limitations of the "heaven, man, and earth" symbolism that is a primary concern of traditional Japanese flower arrangements. In contemporary design, you can take the form of those three central flowers and echo them again for a more complex arrangement. Or you can use only two of the focal flowers, suggesting, but

Contemporary design also means the surprising but effective combination of many different colors, shapes, and textures, eliminating any chance of monotony. This arrangement is a perfect example, with its basically traditional form and contrasting assortment of materials and colors. The exciting red of the sumac is quieted by the pastel shades of the hydrangea. The beauty of the lilies is enhanced as they nestle amidst the fluffy branches of sumac and hydrangea.

Contemporary design means freedom, innovation, and daring for the designer. In this arrangement, you can see the open, lofty new ideas rising from the initial confusion when old, established rules are rejected, as portrayed in the massing of flowers at the bottom of the arrangement. Setting new standards, this centerpiece permits comfortable across-the-table conversation—not over but through the pink rubrum lilies, the white tuberoses, the chincherinchis, and the dendrobium orchids. What better accompaniment is there for pleasant words between friends?

Here, exotic flowers and materials are combined to create a lovely contemporary treatment of Oriental designs. The intense color and form of the heliconia command center stage. However, they are supported by the heart-shaped anthuriums, placed to suggest the "heaven-man-earth" design. The exotics are softened by the delicate oncidium orchids, the montbretia, and the broad ti leaves. The ribbon effect of the ti leaves creates interest and adds weight to the base, a low Oriental bowl filled with marbles. As in most contemporary designs, each flower is given enough space to be enjoyed for its own stunning beauty.

not following, the rules of Oriental design.

Another current trend, also related to the Oriental tradition, is the vegetative design. Here, flowers and foliage are arranged as though they were growing naturally—as though a bit of nature had been lifted out of the earth and placed in a dish. Moss, grasses, branches, stones, bird's nests—almost any devise can be used to enhance the desired effect.

In many other ways, contemporary designs also enable you to bend the old, established rules of floral design. For instance, when flowers are meant to remain on the table during the dinner, they must be arranged so they add to conversation, not deter or inhibit it. By accepted design standards, a centerpiece should be no more than twelve inches high and take up no more than one-quarter of the width of the table. This is a guideline which should always be considered, but with the airiness of contemporary designs today, it can be bent. You could create an arrangement that is thirty-six inches tall, but open enough so guests can see across the table. For very formal dining, tall candelabras and flower arrangements could branch out from above eye level, so conversation may flow easily across the table.

Another example is the deliberate violation of one of the principles of design to emphasize another. The unity of an arrangement could be made less important, tying gerbera daisies with a burlap ribbon to add interest and highlight the contrast in textures. In so many ways, contemporary styling allows you the freedom and encouragement to be bold, innovative, and creative.

Let's look at some contemporary designs and see why they are becoming best-sellers in the floral industry.

Placing flowers at different angles is an element of modern as well as traditional designing. However, contemporary designs use space more freely and deliberately to emphasize each bloom and enrich the overall effect. The heavy branch of cymbidium orchids is placed high, balancing the low, drooping sumac. The arrangement is filled out with gloriosa lilies, firecracker lilies, chincherinchee, and anthurium leaves, and a twisting grape vine is carefully placed to keep the eye moving through the arrangement and to create a sense of unity.
Note also that color is used thoughtfully to balance this arrangement, letting the darker colors carry more weight than the whites or soft pastels.

CHAPTER 8

Seven Step-by-Step Arrangements

Now, let's look into a floral designer's mind-at-work.
Here are seven step-by-step arrangements that will help you to
understand and learn to apply the basics of floral design.

Step 1: *This elegant, but very easy two-step arrangement is a good place to begin examining floral design specifics. In an unintimidating approach, it illustrates a number of the elements and principles of design and can be adapted to a wide variety of flowers.*

Begin by selecting the ingredients for your arrangement—the featured flower type, the accompanying filler, and the container. Be careful that they are all harmonious in shape, texture, and color. In this case, the calla lilies are such an impressive and commanding flower that they need very little more than a few bare branches to enhance them. However, because the floral parts of the design are so minimal, the container plays a larger role, and therefore, must be selected carefully. Here, a heavy crystal vase with an unusual shape and texture complements the graceful lines of the lilies superbly. The bare branches are spread evenly in the container, high enough so the vase is one-third the height of the arrangement and the branches two-thirds, and a strong line is created.

Step 2: *Now, place the calla lilies within the branches. Notice that the flowers are spread so they are evenly balanced, and their heights are staggered for a pleasing form. Also, each flower is given enough space to be fully appreciated. Work the flowers into the branches so the arrangement has a natural rhythm and a unified look.*

Step 1: *With the first few flowers, create the skeleton form of your design. Here, eight open white roses are placed securely into the wet foam—which has been secured in the glass basket and surrounded with moss. The uppermost rose is positioned at twice the height of the container, a good proportion of one-third container to two-thirds flower. Notice that the other roses are positioned so they appear to be radiating into a triangular form.*

Step 2: *Next, white freesias are added, one higher up to assure the correct proportion the others to balance and strengthen the form. At this point the lightest color has been established as dominant in the arrangement, a good basic design plan.*

Step 3: *The medium color should be added next—in this case a blue-lavender combination from the cool side of the spectrum. The lavender of the round scabiosa blossoms harmonizes very well with the blue composite flowers, brodiaea. The three darkest colored flowers—garnet-colored scabiosa—complete the spread of color and balance the form.*

Step 4: *Finally, to blend and unify the look of the arrangement, the delicate caspia is added around the outside, as well as mixed in with the other blooms. Queen Anne's lace is also strategically placed, so that the two wispy flowers and the foliage of all the blossoms work together to fill in the spaces of this arrangement naturally.*

Step 1: *The tall, slim shape of this beautiful container presents many challenges to the designer. It is narrow, so cannot hold many stems, and its shape requires height without breadth. But, with thought and perserverance, though it may take some trial-and-error, a lovely arrangement will emerge from this vase.*

Begin by placing the bare branches at the correct proportional height. Notice once again that the brown stems become the beautiful mechanics of the design, securing and concealing the green stems of the rubrum lilies. The lilies are woven into and spaced evenly among the branches.

Step 2: *Next a smaller, more delicate, and paler lily is incorporated to accent the rubrums. The wispy caspia lightens the overall look, and gives the arrangement a romantic aura.*

Step 3: *Finally, bright pink stock brings boldness and importance to the bouquet, and completes the range of pinks. The white bouvardia contributes the perfect touch of variety, balance, and unity to this wonderful array of color.*

Step 1: *This looks like a particularly complicated and challenging arrangement, but you will be surprised at how easily the design falls into logical steps. First, since a large bouquet is intended, a heavy glass vase with a shape particularly suited to this arrangement is chosen. It has a narrow neck to hold the stems secure, but a wide base so they can spread in enough water to keep them all fresh for a longer time. A bonus consideration is that the wide rim of the mouth makes adding fresh water very easy. The grape vine rings, in fascinating double twists, provide a base and support for the design. The few spreading grasses enhance the natural theme being developed in this design.*

Step 2: *Work the stalks of the monkshood gently into the vines and stems in the vase. Let them fan out to emphasize the open circle form.*

Step 3: *Continuing to construct a "spot of nature," place the cattails high in the arrangement, as they would grow outdoors. Their deep brown color is the perfect balance to the vines, and their rushes echo the color and texture of the rafia bow.*

Step 4: *Now it is the time to insert some color into the basically neutral design. The golden yellow yarrow are positioned in two arches, which follow the circular form. They are also placed in proportion to where they would actually grow in the wild. For a new color twist, insert the pink snapdragons. They are a spike flower, so should stand nearly as high as the monkshood. Notice how effectively they illuminate the blue of the monkshood. Finally, in the center of the arrangement, a lily, a yarrow, and a snapdragon are grouped to become the unifying focal point from which the rest of the natural beauty radiates.*

Step 5: *Form flowers are next, to add body to the outline already created. Again, they are placed proportional to their height in nature, and therefore appear low in the grouping. Orange and yellow marigolds fill out the design beautifully, and are extremely harmonious with the vines and cattails.*

Step 6: *Though the arrangement could be considered complete in the preceding step, a few imaginative finishing touches make it picture perfect and very special. A piece of ivy is twisted around the vine, again just as it would appear in nature. And two bunches of grapes hanging naturally from the vine are included, giving this design European flair. Finally, a second focal lily is positioned to carry the eye gently up into the bursting brilliance of the arrangement.*

Step 1: *Here is an arrangement that changes its shape with each step to build boldly toward the finished product. First, a low ceramic bowl of neutral color is selected, and a pinholder is secured in the bottom with florist's tape. The vibrant orange lilies are placed asymmetrically, but show the influence of Ikebana. A cluster of lilies at the bottom, with one faced forward, establishes the focal point.*

Step 2: *Next, the four calla lilies are positioned prominently. They are one of the most aristocratic flowers, and should always be placed so their lovely gentle shape can be fully appreciated. Here, stems are allowed to arch naturally, as if they were actually growing from the bowl. They are fixed at varied heights to complement the lilies superbly.*

Step 3: *Four yellow irises are added to bring a new form to the design. The bright yellow emerges from the deep orange in an extremely well-balanced and carefully planned strategy. The orange is actually intensified when it is surrounded by sunny yellow.*

Step 4: *The shape of this design is again altered with freesia reaching even further outward to strengthen the developing triangular form. The asymmetry of the original placement of the lilies has been molded in to a vertical shape, which provides the backbone and focal point of the triangle.*

Step 5: *Delicate, white tuberoses subtly fill out the design. Their color is the perfect end to the lightening*

spectrum. And notice that the shape of each kind of flower included harmonizes with the others.

Step 1: *Here is a carefully planned triangular arrangement that incorporates a beautiful variety of flowers and exemplifies the importance of color accents. Begin by selecting a large ginger jar as the container. It will accommodate the open mass arrangement and provide a strong foundation from which to build. Next, the form of the design is established by the short hydrangeas outlining the base of the symmetrical triangle. Bare branches and foliage are added to create the ascending outline of the form and the backdrop of the arrangement. The stems, crisscrossing in the vase, again produce a natural holder for the other flowers, and the mechanics become an integral part of the design. Finally, the foundation color scheme reverberates in each part of the design—the creamy hydrangea with a few green leaves clinging to the brown stem, the foliage with tiny cream-colored flowers, and the brown branches.*

Step: 2: *Now, the tall branch of lilies is added as the focal flower and central color of the design. Their position follows the triangular form, and also unifies the design by highlighting the pink shades in the hydrangea. Notice that several buds are included so that they will open later and keep the arrangement looking fresh.*

Step 3: *The delicate yellow freesia are carefully woven into the design. Special care is taken not to bend their stems. Their bright hue brings the eye back to the center of the lilies, and illuminates another dimension of the color spectrum in the hydrangeas themselves. Additionally, freesia will contribute a lovely spring fragrance.*

Step 4: *The design is filled out with two more kinds of flowers. Both the white gerbera daisies and the dendrobium orchids sustain the cream/yellow color scheme, and the touch of pink on the stem and flowers of the orchids also complements the lilies. Now that the arrangement is complete, it is obvious that each flower was lovingly selected to accentuate the exquisite lilies.*

Step 1: *Designing the perfect arrangement takes a little planning and a lot of patience. In an innovative twist, this design begins with a framework of grape vines. Arched in three rings, they are wide enough to balance the round glass bowl, and are extended into the container to act as a natural pinholder for the stems of the other flowers. The vines are secured with a bit of unobtrusive green florist's wire.*

Step 2: *Next, the four lilies are placed low in the arrangement, one within each ring and another in the center of the design. These become the accent or focal flowers. The stems are crisscrossed through the grape vines in the bowl so they are sure to stay in place.*

Step 3: *Now, the delicate montbretia flowers are arranged around the lilies, at a proportional height to balance the arrangement. Again, the stems are carefully woven into the mechanics of the bowl to provide even more stability for the grouping. Note that though the montbretia blooms are slender and small, their intense color lets them hold their own next to the magnificent lilies. However, the montbretia make the variety of orange shades in the lilies come alive. This reflects just how carefully these complementary flowers have been selected.*

Step 4: *The color spectrum and the form of this design is filled out with several types of complementary blossoms. The delicate, upward reaching oncidium orchids establish the width of the asymmetrical triangle. With the bright yellow tansy, they intensify the color in the center of the lilies. The light accent of*

the cream-colored freesia is positioned to keep the eye moving around the lilies in a steady, circling rhythm. Each element of this loose, natural arrangement is harmoniously colored so as to focus on the beauty of the central and featured flower, the lily.

CHAPTER 9

Line Arrangements: Flowers and Branches

*A*ll flower arrangements, no matter how casual in appearance, are inspired by geometric lines. The line provides the outline of the form you are creating, whether straight, for a square or triangular arrangement, or curved, for an oval or spherical one. The line provides the framework or outline for your design.

In today's high-fashion designs line is more than an outline of form. We use line for accent, originality, impact, a study in color. This is achieved with strong horizontal or vertical lines, or possibly diagonal. Branches of pussy willow or forsythia thrust upward, or they may jut out to form a diagonal across the entire arrangement. Or bamboo shoots

This arrangement is a beautiful harmony of color and far-reaching lines. The eucalyptus branches outline the triangular form, but also seem to continue on to lofty heights. Their deep green color accents the lovely pink of the rambling roses and the rosa lilies. The soft lavender of the freesia also accentuates the radiating lines of the design, while the Queen Anne's lace strengthens the triangular form with the feminine look of lace.

The roses form the dominant lines in this bridal bouquet, but all the flowers and branches radiate outward, which leaves the impression that the form extends beyond the perimeters of the flowers themselves.

The dendrobium orchids form a strong line that sweeps from top to bottom of this bridal bouquet. It commands attention, yet the grace of the anemones and waxflowers supports the cascade of beauty.

may be placed horizontally at the base of an arrangement for a far-reaching effect.

The growing emphasis on line reflects our interest in the effective use of space. High ceilings, especially in contemporary homes, call for proportionately tall arrangements. In a room with ten-foot-high ceilings, there are about seven feet of wall space above the furniture that can be decorated with pictures, art objects, shelves, or possibly vertical lines of flowering branches placed in a tall urn. Branches of flowering quince or apple blossoms would provide color in the spring. Or dramatic cattails, or branches of ruddy oak leaves will bring the loveliness of fall inside.

In another setting, a horizontal line of holly and evergreens across a fireplace mantel is pleasing, and the effect—especially since it is at about eye level—is very rewarding. Or offset an angle arrangement with a horizontal line. Carry through the line at the base of the design to highlight a buffet or sideboard. Place an arrangement at the end of a table and run a horizontal line design down the center of the table with manzanita wood and candles for a chic but elegant look.

When choosing flowers for different line accents in an arrangement, I like to use them according to the way they grow. Gladiolus, for instance, should always be used for vertical lines. Other spike flowers include snapdragons, delphiniums, liatris, and stock. Round flowers, called form flowers, are placed below the spike flowers. They are great for horizontal and diagonal lines. The taller ones might be long-stemmed roses, or carnations, or dahlias. Lower down you might have gerbera daisies, dianthus, statice, and assorted foliage. The shorter the natural stem, the closer they should be to the base of the arrangement. Of course, many of today's great floral artists break all these "rules"— but the rules are helpful as a guideline.

At first glance, this all-white centerpiece seems so neutral that whatever else you would use on the table would dominate it. However, a burgundy tablecloth and napkins would provide a beautiful backdrop for the white flowers, emphasizing the intricate design of this arrangement. Connect all the like flowers here, and you will see the gently crossing lines they form. For example, the hydrangeas sweep up to the right, and the dendrobium orchids arch in a crescent across them. You begin to see that every flower here has a deliberate and important role.

Delicate, airy, and in a color that is wonderfully complementary to the face, this narrow corsage surprisingly slenderizes its wearer. The line of dendrobium orchids is nicely balanced so that the width becomes less important than the length, emphasizing the strong line of the design. The thin satin ribbon, flowing in and around the blossoms, is in perfect balance with the flowers and is the only filler needed.

Lines are the basis of most corsage designs. Many form a curving trail over the shoulder to accentuate the beauty of the wearer. Others are small, lightweight, and worn perched on the shoulder. In this design, two lines of light pink roses crisscross over the shoulder and are filled out with a narrow ribbon of a deeper shade. A simple but elegant corsage, it is appropriate for a formal occasion or just for everyday.

Other natural materials can be used for line and accent: manzanita wood, birch branches, sweet-gum branches, salt cedar, greasewood, mitsumata branches, wisteria vine, twisted yonagi, cattails, panchu spring, cane coil and cone, cane spring, wire grass, and wild oats. In fact, you can use any growing plant to create the effect you want. These materials add interest and a new dimension to your basic form.

Most corsage designs are made up of definite lines, usually a row of flowers that curves up and over the shoulder towards the face. The arch softens and complements the face by lining it with beautiful blooms of enticing colors. Remember that the line of flowers is just one of many to consider in a corsage. The hairline, the neck and shoulder line of the dress, and the jawline of the face should all converge to enhance the wearer.

Just as any arrangement, a corsage can be specifically designed for one person or for a very special occasion. A corsage worn to a dinner should be small and simple, with little fragrance so it won't be overbearing or ostentatious during the meal. However, a corsage for a formal event can be more daring and dramatic. Begin a line of roses at the back neck of a formal gown, and wrap it over and down the shoulder to the front. Or create a crescent, like an inverted smile, to adorn one side at the hip of the gown. But always make sure that your design is not intrusive or too elaborate to allow the wearer to move comfortably and freely.

Take a look at the lines in the arrangements in this chapter and use them as a starting-off point. From here you can develop your own self-expression, your own floral style and image.

Color is the primary ingredient in this "French bouquet," but none of the elements or principles of design have been neglected. The soft, gentle, pastel colors blend in an analogous color combination. But each flower is allowed enough space to be enjoyed and appreciated separately. The pink lilies, lavender scabiosa, and caspia complement each other in a mix of textures, and are filled out with accents of blue and lavender from the delphinium and freesia. The hues are further softened by white tulips and Queen Anne's lace. Small pieces of ivy unify the arrangement and complete the balance of this technically superb and esthetically pleasing centerpiece.

Sunny yellow tulips look quite at home in this flowerpot centerpiece. Their different ages, shown by the tight and open forms, emphasize the natural look of this design and create a stronger, more effective, focal point. Together, the lines of the blooms form a striking triangle. Three shell pink belladonna lilies burst from the center and reach to the height of the arrangement, forming another triangle on top. The slender pink wildflowers, known as "smartweed," lend action and a unique contrast and, along with the galax leaves placed low in the arrangement, fill it out and enhance its "spot of nature" theme.

Study this garden arrangement carefully and appreciate the many ways lines can be used in a design. First, the bare branches form two diagonals originating in the vase, and they establish the height of the arrangement. The two blue agapanthus suggest another line, and the pink alstroemeria, a strong triangle. Finally, the bright goldenrod add a gentle curve over and through the design. All of these lines harmonize to keep the eye moving through this natural-looking, evocative bouquet, to appreciate each blossom for its own beauty, and to witness the relationship between the flowers that enhances them even more.

CHAPTER 10

Dried Arrangements

As a painter may use watercolor or acrylic, and work on canvas or cardboard, so a floral artist may use different mediums. The same principles of design are used in dried flower arrangements as in fresh ones; only the mechanics vary.

Instead of using water-absorbing foam to hold the stems, you use a foam product made especially for dried arrangements. The most popular product is called "Sahara,™" a spongy-looking plastic that actually has a very firm consistency. "Sahara™" is designed to repel water, to keep the dried flowers crisp. Since it is dry, it can be anchored to your container with glue instead of tape. And it can be covered with the materials described in Chapter 6, "Mechanics", or with dried moss, baby's breath, sugarbush, or broom bloom. Wire, tape, and picks are used as they are with fresh flowers.

Many people think of dried arrangements as being traditional in style—often Early American or Victorian. But in fact, dried flowers are mixed with silk or fresh flowers today for a very fashionable look.

Silk flowers are very chic, and are finding their way into every aspect of interior design. Although they lack the fragrance and ephemeral excitement of fresh flowers, they have a value and flexibility all their own.

They are bent more easily than fresh flowers, so they can be used more artfully. You can create angle and rhythm in a design more successfully, and with their wide range of never-fading color, they will spice up the look of a bland all-dried arrangement.

Silk floral arrangements can be placed in spots that do not have enough light to maintain a living plant. And they can be used as permanent accents to carry out the color scheme of a room. A dainty silk flower enclosed in a glass dome, or a massive freestanding arrangement in the corner of the room, will add color, balance, and harmony to any interior design all year round.

All-dried arrangements, as well as combinations of silk and dried, and fresh and dried, have a place in today's interiors.

This lovely arrangement defies any preconceived notions that all dried flowers are brown. The bleached branches here contrast precisely with the spiral leaves of the eucalyptus and add drama with their fascinatingly gnarled reach. The smaller dried flowers—some bleached and some left natural—provide a light but full effect. The pink rattail statice blends perfectly with the shaded vase, completing the exquisite color harmony of the design. A tall cylinder vase was selected so there will be no chance that it will topple.

Drying Flowers

There are many ways of drying flowers, some better suited to certain types of flowers than others. Go ahead and experiment—you'll undoubtedly have some happy surprises.

One technique involves covering the flower with a desiccant (a drying medium) in which it stays until it has dried completely. This can be silica gel (available at craft and garden shops), sand (rinsed thoroughly of all salty residue if you use beach sand), or even kitty litter. Weak stems should be removed and replaced with wire stems inserted into the base of the blossom. Woody stems can remain on, but all leaves should be removed from the stem. (If a dried stem breaks, mend it with wire, a floral pick, or even a toothpick, and cover it in floral tape of a matching color.) Pour an inch of the dry material into a container, and place the flowers, heads down in most cases, on it. Some flowers maintain their shape better when dried head up or laid horizontally. You can discover this by asking your florist, or just by trial and error. Cover the flowers with the drying material, and if you are using gel, seal the can with duct tape. A simple flower (single petals), like cosmos and field daisies, should dry in three or four days. A compound flower (layers of petals) like a carnation could take a week to ten days. The container should be kept in a dry place—an attic or closet. Never leave it in a damp garage or cellar, which could result in mold and mildew, in addition to slowing down the process. Remove the drying medium carefully, dusting the petals with a soft paintbrush. Remember that the dried petals will be very brittle. Now you are ready to arrange your dried flowers.

Using the microwave oven to dry your flowers with a desiccant, or freeze-drying

A woven vine basket is a striking container for an all-dried arrangement. Many of the fascinating ingredients in this design can be collected in the wild. Some have been picked fresh and dried by one of the methods described, and others, like the beautiful seedpod in the top center of the arrangement, have been left to mature in the fields. This design is classic: The tall dock are positioned first to establish the correct proportions of the arrangement, then a wide assortment of dried flowers is spread evenly all around and at various heights to fill out the bouquet.

Who said wreaths should only be hung on the front door at Christmas? This colorful wreath is appropriate both inside and outdoors. First, the base is formed by tying an assortment of dried weeds onto a wire frame. All the other material—pods, seed heads, cinnamon sticks, and dried flowers—can be glued or wired into place, or attached to floral picks and stuck securely into the weed-covered wire frame. The warm colors are very welcoming, especially in a setting of Early American decor.

them are much more complicated processes. The timing for both precedures must be measured to the second, and the results are very unpredictable. Because of this, flowers are dried in this manner less often, and we do not encourage you to try.

Another, older, process is even simpler. This is air-drying. It holds the color best, and air-dried flowers last longer. Gather your choice of garden flowers or attractive weeds and wildflowers into small bunches, and tie

the items together with string or a rubber band. Hang the bunches upside-down in a dark, dry, warm location. An attic is probably best; a damp basement worst. Allow the air to dry them naturally. You can observe the change almost daily as the moisture leaves the flowers. In ideal conditions, the process could take a week, but it's more likely to be two weeks or even longer, depending on the climate and the flowers themselves. Be patient—it's worth it! And don't be reluctant

A wreath of assorted evergreen cones is time-consuming to assemble, but very versatile and rewarding to display. The two easiest techniques are to wire or glue the cones onto a wooden straw, wire, or Styrofoam wreath frame. Cones come in an amazing variety of sizes, colors, and shapes, and you will have no trouble creating a unified but fascinating design. Depending on the season when you display it, you could add an orange burlap ribbon to suggest fall, or a red one for Christmastime.

to try all kinds of flowers—many types will work better as dried flowers than you expect.

Many of the flowers in your garden will produce beautiful seedpods after their flowers have finished. Don't pinch off every dead flower, and you will discover some fascinating stages of development and wonderful materials to work with. For instance, the lily and the tulip both unexpectedly produce curving heads. Dipping seedpods in varnish will sometimes help them hold their lovely

form, as well as deepening their color and adding a dramatic sheen. But no matter what, watch for seedheads and use them in surprising new ways.

Storing Dried Flowers

You'll probably want to store your dried arrangements in the summer months when fresh flowers are abundant. To do so, wrap them loosely in newspaper and place them

117

in cardboard boxes. Do not wrap them in plastic; you want them to have air around them so mildew won't form, and plastic will create damaging humidity. It's fine to store them in a warm location, so long as it is as dry as possible. Store them in a dark area, away from sunlight, so the colors don't fade before you use them.

Buying Dried Flowers

Dried flowers, loose and in arrangements, are widely available and are not expensive—and easier, or course, than trying to dry your own. No longer considered a fall item, they are available year round. With the introduction of unusual dried materials from Africa, Australia, and other corners of the world, new and exciting items are available on the market. Their intriguing shapes and colors allow floral designers to be more innovative. Try repens star, monkeypods, sponge mushrooms, or ming moss for a new look in your dried arrangements. Jinga pods, chico choke, okra pods, and the popular lotus pods are great for accent lines.

For a truly dramatic effect, you might want to use bleached materials. Wild oats, thistles, wheat, eryanthus, sugarbush, ferns, and hydrangeas can all be bleached white or off-white. (Bleaching is a trial-and-error process if you want to try it yourself. Some materials need full-strength bleach, some a mixture of fifty percent bleach, fifty percent water. Soak the material in the bleach mixture until it reaches the lightness you would like. Remove it and rinse it in clean water to stop the process. Some take fifteen minutes to bleach out, some a day or longer.)

If you are interested in seeing one of the largest selections of dried materials, write to the Knud Nielsen Company (see Sources, page 169) and ask for their catalogue full of ideas; or they can direct you to a nearby source for these materials.

An alternative to fresh flowers—and one that is guaranteed to remain looking impeccably fresh—is a silk bouquet. Here, and on the previous page, are two small baskets, enticingly filled with silk flowers, branches, and fresh baby's breath, perfect for a flower girl to carry down the aisle. Today silk flowers have an amazingly fresh and realistic look, and come in an astonishing array of colors and varieties.

CHAPTER 11

Miniatures

When is an arrangement a miniature? Well, in a flower show, the limit might be 3 inches—meaning that it can't be larger than that in any direction, height or width. This is a real challenge for the contestant. Where do I find a vase the size of a thimble? And where do I find flowers about one-third the size of the vase—or less? These amazingly tiny arrangements obviously require patience, care with detail, and experience.

A more popular flower-show size is five inches, but when you are making miniature arrangements for your own pleasure, you can certainly extend the "rules" to an eight-inch maximum. Miniatures may be frustrating when you're having to conform to judges' rules, but they are lots of fun to create for yourself or to give to others.

The important thing to keep in mind when designing your miniature is that however small it may be, the final presentation must still follow the basic principles of design. Lack of size doesn't mean you can overlook the six principles of balance, harmony, rhythm, unity, scale, or accent. The five elements of unity, color, line, form, and space are also just as important as in large designs. The two aspects that are hardest to maintain in miniatures are scale and space.

The tendency with these tiny arrangements is to overstuff them and forget to leave space so that we can enjoy each blossom. Your perfect little creation is even more wonderful when we can clearly see the scale of the different components.

Scale includes the relationship of the sizes of the flowers to one another, of the flowers to the container, and of the arrangement to its setting. A miniature arrangement in the center of a dining-room table is out of scale, but a miniature on a serving tray or on a small glass shelf in the bathroom would be in scale. Generally, the container should take up about one-third of the overall size, the flowers two-thirds. As for the flowers themselves, the guideline is that the width of the flower should be no more than one-third the height of the container. Half an inch seems to be the maximum diameter of a flower used in true miniature arrangements.

It's not easy to find such small flowers, and blossoms that seem small in your regular-size arrangements will be too big for a miniature. One solution is to use composite flowers—blossoms that are made up of many small flowers. Liatris, for example, is a spike consisting of many small side flowers, ideal for miniatures. Queen Anne's Lace, a wildflower, is another source of tiny individual flowers. So is a blossom of candytuft. Other composite flowers that could be separated and used this way are lilac, phlox, ageratum, some violets, many small berries, heather,

Miniature arrangements are lots of fun to make. You need only a few flowers, and you can use your imagination to discover ways to use parts of a composite flower. The end product will fit in unexpected spaces, surprising the viewer with a burst of color and fragrant joy. Here, an arrangement of a few roses, waxflowers, and blue brodiaea makes a statement of delicate simplicity.

kalanchoe, yarrow, and oncidium orchids. Searching and discovering what you can use is part of the fun. Don't forget that the foliage you use must also be in scale.

Individual mini arrangements placed at each guest's place would create a warm welcome at a dinner party, especially if they were derived from the main centerpiece and could be taken home as a gift. Of course, nothing could be classier than a miniature in one of Fabergé's fabulous royal Easter eggs, but failing that, how about your own collection of small colored glass vases and bottles? Place a couple of them in a sunny window and the color of the glass will bounce all around the room.

There are myriad imaginative ways to use miniature flowers. With a touch of glue you can attach them to earrings, cufflinks, or to the buttons down the front of a dress or shirt. They are fun accenting the corners of a pair of eyeglasses, or the buckles of a pair of shoes. You can even sprinkle little blossoms through your hair. How about a miniature corsage for a baby's christening or first birthday, or a small cluster of flowers attached to a comb for a child's hair? Did you ever try putting a blossom on a ring?

Dried miniatures can have personal meaning, too. A young woman's first corsage could be taken apart, dried, and made into a miniature; cover it with a glass dome and you'll have a keepsake of a happy memory. The same thing could be done with a prom bouquet, to be placed on a special spot in a curio cabinet. And of course a selection from a wedding bouquet arranged in an engraved champagne glass could also become a small dried arrangement and a lasting keepsake.

Small figurines, tiny vases, ceramic shoes —all can be placed on windowsills, in cabinets, or in shadow boxes and filled with colorful dried flowers, a cluster of bleached gypsophila, or small arrangements of fresh flowers. Once you start experimenting, you'll come up with more and more ideas, and you'll find yourself arranging flowers for every nook and cranny.

The size of this blue bud vase is perfect for a miniature arrangement. The opening will hold only a few carefully selected blossoms—in this case lavender orchids and a single blue agapanthus, which will soothe the viewer after a hectic day.

THERE ARE MANY KINDS OF FLOWERS THAT HAVE SPECIFIC MINIATURE VARIETIES. AMONG THEM ARE:

Roses

Carnations

Gladiolus

Orchids

Marigolds

Zinnias

Irises

Narcissus

Day lilies

Dahlias

SOME USEFUL COMPOSITE FLOWERS ARE:

Baby's breath

Statice

Pompom chrysanthemums

Alstroemeria

Queen Anne's lace

Candytuft

Lilacs

Phlox

Ageratum

Violets

Bittersweet

Heather

Floribunda roses

Yarrow

Oncidium orchids

Bouvardia

Liatris

ASK YOUR FLORIST ABOUT OTHERS

CHAPTER 12

Natural Accessories

*T*here is no doubt that flowers themselves are beautiful enough to be appreciated. Their fragrances, colors, forms, are a silent language of esthetic value. However, there are times when you will want to enhance a flower's beauty with natural accessories.

We have already mentioned numerous dried and silk accessories which you can use in your arrangements—lotus pods, branches, ferns, and much more. But if you just open your eyes and your mind you will see all kinds of things that will look terrific in your designs. There is a new floral trend, for instance, called the "European" or "Flemish Country" look, that incorporates fresh fruits and vegetables as highlights and as a celebration of living things. Green and red peppers, purple eggplant, any of the variety of squashes and gourds, cucumbers, artichokes, or mushrooms will all add a fascinating dimension of color and texture to your arrangement. Cut the tops off the peppers, or the hearts out of the artichokes, and they will make wonderful candle holders. Or you can even fill them with miniature blossoms.

There are also many ways to use fruit in flower arranging. Oranges and apples in a fall arrangement of earthy-colored flowers will emphasize that it is the season of the harvest. For a luncheon or afternoon buffet, cut lemons and oranges in halves or quarters. Put them on floral picks and place them low in an arrangement of bright flowers. Your bouquet will have a lovely citrus fragrance, as well as bright bursts of color.

For a summer party, cut a watermelon in half and use it as a container. The melon will hold flowers almost as well as floral foam will, and your guests will enjoy eating the other half of the melon.

Enhance a cool, simple dessert of cantaloupe or honeydew with a small Vanda orchid in the middle or on the plate. Or cut a pineapple in half lengthwise, then slice it and place a vibrant "Claudia" gerbera daisy at each end for the perfect finishing touch.

Here is a tropical centerpiece which features unusual flowers and stunning natural accessories. The "Queen" protea, centered in the arrangement, commands immediate attention. The three pincushion protea then carry the eye around the arrangement, and are interestingly softened by the drumstick allium, the dendrobium orchids, and the freesia. The decorator pink pineapple emphasizes the tropical feel of the design, and the apples and grapes suggest the theme of the abundance of nature. The whole bouquet sits in a sturdy ginger jar, stable enough to hold the extra-heavy ingredients, and it is all tied up with a raffia bow, the perfect natural touch.

The natural accessories here accent but do not overpower the brilliant colors and fascinating shapes of
the parrot tulips, blue delphinium, orange lilies, and bright yellow tansies. It is a perfect summer picnic

centerpiece with vibrant color to stimulate the appetite. Remember that fruit and vegetables are appropriate only in an arrangement to be used in a dining setting, such as the dining room or kitchen nook.

Congratulations on the new job! And say it with more than flowers. Use actual gifts as ingredients in your

floral design, and the flowers as the wrapping.

Natural accessories can be used imaginatively to set the stage for an evening of pleasant dining. Here, a variety of brightly colored fruits and vegetables look lovelier than could ever be imagined and will tease

anyone's appetite. Candles flicker with cunning and elegance from the centers of artichokes. This array reminds one of the abundance of the earth and the graciousness of a hospitable host.

There are hundreds of ways to use fruit and vegetables in food presentation. Fruits, vegetables, and flowers are all living things and they belong together.

But don't pass by other natural accessories, such as driftwood, stones, cypress knees, coral, and shells. Empty bird's nests will give your arrangement a landscape appearance, as if you'd brought a piece of the outside in. In fact, if you walk through a wooded area, along a beach, or on a mountain path, you are sure to discover many unexpected, but wonderful things you can bring in to add to your arrangements.

Don't be afraid to use flowers in unexpected ways as a secondary accessory—as the bow on a package, for example, or the rosettes on top of a cake. A blossom may add the final touch of life and beauty.

You can also incorporate all kinds of nonnatural objects. For instance, a bottle of champagne can peek from behind the blooms of an anniversary bouquet. Or a small gift, such as a piece of jewelry or the keys to a car, can become the focal point of an arrangement. In fact, you can spotlight almost any item you want to if you design your arrangement accordingly.

But, here is a note of caution. Always use accessories with discrimination. An excessive amount of extras will clutter and detract from—rather than add to—your design. There is a thin line between appropriateness and excess, and many designers believe that "less is always better."

When choosing your accessories, keep in mind the six principles of design discussed in Chapter 4. For instance, carefully consider the size of the accessory and make sure it fits the scale of your design. It should neither overpower the flowers in the arrangement nor be hidden by them. Also make sure the accessory does not violate the unity of the arrangement. For example, a piece of driftwood may not belong in a bouquet of lilies, and an artichoke may look out of place with roses and carnations. Don't be afraid to use accessories, but choose them carefully and use them only to enrich the design.

Here's a new presentation for a collection of bath accessories—tucked into a basket and accompanied by pink roses and waxflowers. A lacy ribbon completes the design and invites you to relax in the tub.

Wine, glasses, candles, and roses belong together in a romantic anniversary gift. One red rose cannot be misunderstood, but it is eloquently echoed in the color from the strawberries and the wine label.

How can you invigorate the traditional picnic basket of wine, fruit, cheese, and bread? Add a few brightly colored posies, and your package becomes a very thoughtful gift for a special friend.

CHAPTER 13

The Arranger's Garden

*I*t is very satisfying to be able to look out a window and enjoy the results of your toil in the garden. Digging in the earth, planting in it, is being as close to nature as one can be. Watching the new life return in the spring is miraculous. And with spring comes the time to plan the garden. It is ideal to have flowers blooming from early spring until the end of fall. Give some thought now to choices for your flower garden that will provide color for an entire year—growing outside, and in arrangements inside. This is also a good time to plan for the natural accessories you can grow in your part of the world, to use later in your flower arranging.

There are plants for every possible outdoor condition—whether the soil is wet or dry, heavy or light, whether your spot is in sun, partial sun, or shade. Ask at your local nursery, florist, or garden center for suggestions. Or send for some of the catalogs that "blossom" in the spring (one of the best is put out by Wayside Gardens—see Sources, page 169).

Planting bulbs in the fall will provide spring's first welcome. Any variety of daffodil will be cheery after a cold winter, but be sure to include "King Alfred," a classic yellow, and "Mt. Hood," a regal bloom of purest white. If you want the "orchid" of daffodils, try "Pink Glory"—it's dazzling. Other bulbs to consider would be some of the dozens of tulips: "Moonstruck," a light yellow; "Valentine," an exceptional beauty of rose and white; "Angelique," a unique combination of pink and cream; "Elizabeth Arden," a salmon-pink Darwin hybrid; and especially the bright cherry-red "Supreme." There are so many new tulips, bright, fringed, tall, short, early bloomers, and late bloomers. You have your choice of hundreds of flowers.

The best part of cultivating your own garden is sharing your success with others. Here, a few prize specimens are gathered enchantingly with a bow: blue and lavender delphinium, orange and alba lilies, painted asters, and agapanthus. Together, they are a lovely, living gift for a very special friend.

Witness this simple but extremely beautiful arrangement, which comes straight from your own garden. A few fluffy white hydrangea blossoms are placed in a round glass vase. Bursting from the center are ten open "Champagne" roses, testimony to the natural beauty of flowers. This cool, comforting arrangement reflects the ease and relaxation so many people find while working in their gardens.

Try devoting a small area to anemone bulbs. And allium, both "Drumstick" and "Giganteum"—you'll be amazed at this unique flower, which can also be dried for winter enjoyment. Add some small crocuses in another area of the garden. They bloom much earlier than any other bulbs. For a tall flower against a fence, try eremurus (foxtail lily). It grows as high as three feet and the sunny yellow or pink flowers last well when cut. And include another spot in the garden for a dozen or two sweet-scented hyacinths. They are without a doubt the most fragrant of all spring flowers.

Plant as many perennials as possible; these plants last from year to year, and they continue to get bigger and better. Some favorites to consider are peonies ("Chiffon Parfait"), bearded iris (especially "Camelot Rose," "Gala Madrid," or "Cranberry Ice"). Oriental poppies are gorgeous and easy to grow; try "Big Jim," "Harvest Moon," or "Blue Moon." Other choice perennials include lily of the valley, columbine, gaillardia, Shasta daisies, digitalis (foxglove), gypsophila (baby's breath), liatris, phlox (possibly "Sandra" or "Progress"), monarda, lupin, sedums ("Autumn Joy"), and astilbe ("Fanal" or "Rheinland"). A tritoma plant (red hot poker) provides exciting color for your arrangements.

Spring is also the time for planting shrubs you can use for their flowers or foliage. Azaleas (especially "Helen Curtis" and "Maybelle") are covered with spring bloom. Pyracantha (preferably "Teton") produces bunches of bright orange berries in the fall. A willow tree would provide curly branches, and forsythia and japonica are other good additions. You can cut their branches for Oriental or contemporary designs, and they'll grow even bushier after the trimming.

Summer calls for annuals, which must be replaced every year, to fill out your perennial garden. Add red or pink geraniums along the border of a path or in a sunny location near a window so you can look outside and enjoy their brilliance. Plant colorful petunias, prolific impatiens, blue ageratum, assorted coleus, white allysum. Visit your garden center, ask questions, and find out which annuals will do best in your garden.

When fall returns you can add colorful chrysanthemums here and there—some are hardy enough to carry over from year to year. Many summer annuals will bloom into the late fall. For those of us in the temperate zone regions, now is the time to make up a few dried arrangements, full of summer memories. You can also bring assorted evergreen branches indoors and continue to enjoy the color and pleasant aroma of outdoors as winter sets in. Then, bring in branches of forsythia, japonica, quince, or pussy willow and watch them every day as they come into early bloom and their leaves unfurl. It really helps to shorten the cold winter.

December belongs to the poinsettia plant. Most of the new varieties will last a couple of months inside, so you can enjoy that bright accent of color in your window for a long time. The red is still the most exciting, but you also have the choice of white, pink, and marble (pink and white combination)—and now there's a new mini poinsettia, great for boutonnieres, corsages, and holiday bridal bouquets.

What we didn't plant this year we will consider for next spring. Maybe we'll add a holly tree, preferably "Blue Stallion" or "China Girl," to provide some Christmas greens for next year. The broad leaf of the rhododendron is a must this year; it will be an addition I can use in my traditional designs. For curves and extra height I'll need a Scotch broom plant, and for my Ikebana class a pink dogwood and a stand of bamboo. (I'm gradually using more and more of my lawn to plant flowers and shrubs, and I'm enjoying it!) Now, before May I want to plant twelve or more hybrid tea and grandiflora roses, and maybe "Cupcake," a delicate pink miniature rose. I'd like to include the fragrant orange-red "Dolly Parton"—maybe two of them. "Brandy" is a burnt-orange color. The dainty light pink "Michele Meillant" is a true aristocrat of roses. I'll need a climber, and "Spectra" is the newest gold and crimson color available. I must have a "Peace"—it's the finest hybrid tea rose ever produced. Then there is "Royal Highness," glorious "Tropicana," yellow "Gold Medal," deliciously scented white "Lightnin'," "Friendship," "Queen Elizabeth," and so many more. Maybe next year I'll have to add another rose garden and another twelve new varieties!

The garden seems full right now, but each year I find something new and useful, and naturally I will find room for it in my garden of pleasure.

APPENDIX 1

Flowers and Their Seasons

ACACIA

BOTANICAL NAME
Acacia podalyriifolia; Leguminosae

SEASON
September through October

COLORS
Yellow

SPECIAL INSTRUCTIONS
A long-lasting flower; striking alone

AGAPANTHUS

BOTANICAL NAME
Agapanthus africanus; Liliaceae

SEASON
May through October

COLORS
Predominantly blue and white;
also yellow and dark lilac

SPECIAL INSTRUCTIONS
A long-lasting flower; dramatic;
good for contemporary designs

ALSTROEMERIA
or
PERUVIAN LILY

AMARYLLIS

BOTANICAL NAME
Alstroemeria pelegrina; Liliaceae

SEASON
All year

COLORS
Yellow, rust, orange, gold, red, rose,
pink, light yellow

SPECIAL INSTRUCTIONS
A long-lasting flower;
multi-flowering; remove most leaves
from the stem

BOTANICAL NAME
Amaryllis belladonna;
Amaryllidaceae

SEASON
February through December

COLORS
Many colors

SPECIAL INSTRUCTIONS
Mixes well with poppies, anemones,
and irises; also beautiful alone

ANEMONE
or
WINDFLOWER

ANTHURIUM

BOTANICAL NAME
Anemone cornaria; Ranunculaceae

SEASON
January through mid-September

COLORS
White, pink, red, purple, lavender

SPECIAL INSTRUCTIONS
Not a long-lasting flower; follow
preconditioning process carefully;
keep at cool temperature

BOTANICAL NAME
Anthurium andreanum; Araceae

SEASON
All year

COLORS
"Guatemala"—red, "Jamaica"—white

SPECIAL INSTRUCTIONS
One of the five exotic flowers;
long-lasting and needs no
refrigeration

ASTER

BOTANICAL NAME
Aster novi-belgii; Compositae

SEASON
August through November

COLORS
White, pink, lavender, purple

SPECIAL INSTRUCTIONS
Strong form flower; a long-lasting
flower; vivid colors; mixes well with
irises, snapdragons, marigolds,
zinnias, lilies; stem may need
to be wired

BABY'S BREATH

BOTANICAL NAME
Gypsophila paniculata;
Caryophyllaceae

SEASON
All year

COLORS
White, pink

SPECIAL INSTRUCTIONS
Good drying plant; creates a wispy
effect in arrangements;
excellent filler

BACHELOR'S BUTTON
or
CORNFLOWER

BIRD-OF-PARADISE

BOTANICAL NAME
Centaurea cyanus; Compositae

BOTANICAL NAME
Strelitzia reginae; Strelitziaceae

SEASON
May through November

SEASON
All year

COLORS
White, pink, blue

COLORS
Orange

SPECIAL INSTRUCTIONS
Delicate stem; not a long-lasting
flower; fades in excessively bright
light; flower dries well; replace stem
with wire before drying

SPECIAL INSTRUCTIONS
One of the five exotic flowers;
a long-lasting flower

BRODIAEA

BOTANICAL NAME
Brodiaea elegans; Liliaceae

SEASON
April through October

COLORS
Lavender, white

SPECIAL INSTRUCTIONS
Mixes well with other bulb-blooming
flowers, such as tulips, irises,
and anemones

CARNATION
(miniature)

BOTANICAL NAME
Dianthus caryophyllus hybride;
Caryophyllaceae

SEASON
All year

COLORS
Many colors

SPECIAL INSTRUCTIONS
A long-lasting flower; arrange in bud
vase or glass vase 6″ to 9″ tall; mixes
well with brodiaea, pompom
chrysanthemums, irises, and
baby's breath

CARNATION
(standard)

CELOSIA

BOTANICAL NAME
Dianthus caryophyllus hybride;
Caryophyllaceae

SEASON
All year

COLORS
Many colors: "White Sim"—white,
"Charmeur"—lavender,
"Lena"—orange,
"Pallas Londorga"—yellow

SPECIAL INSTRUCTIONS
A long-lasting flower

BOTANICAL NAME
Celosia argentea plumosa;
Amaranthaceae

SEASON
Early spring through winter

COLORS
Mostly red, yellow, orange

SPECIAL INSTRUCTIONS
A long-lasting flower; versatile filler

CHRYSANTHEMUM

CLOVER

BOTANICAL NAME
Chrysanthemum morifolium;
Compositae

SEASON
All year

COLORS
Many colors

SPECIAL INSTRUCTIONS
A long-lasting flower; available in all
sizes, from 1″ to 7″ in diameter

BOTANICAL NAME
Trifolium; Leguminosae

SEASON
Summer through early fall

COLORS
Red, white

SPECIAL INSTRUCTIONS
Not a long-lasting flower; dries well

COSMOS

BOTANICAL NAME
Cosmos bipinnatus; Compositae

SEASON
Late summer into fall

COLORS
White, rose, orange, red, yellow

SPECIAL INSTRUCTIONS
Not a long-lasting flower; a light airy
blossom; mixes well with zinnias
and marigolds

CYMBIDIUM ORCHIDS

BOTANICAL NAME
Cymbidium orchis; Orchidaceae

SEASON
All year

COLORS
Many colors

SPECIAL INSTRUCTIONS
Flowers are irregular in shape: each
has 3 sepals and 3 petals, with only 2
petals alike; a strong focal flower;
mixes well with other orchids;
many sizes

DAHLIA

DELPHINIUM
or
LARKSPUR

BOTANICAL NAME
Dahlia hybriden; Compositae

SEASON
June through October

COLORS
Many colors

SPECIAL INSTRUCTIONS
Mixes well with gladiolus, liatris,
delphinium, and asters

BOTANICAL NAME
Delphinium grandiflorum;
Ranunculaceae

SEASON
May to August

COLORS
White, dark blue, lavender

SPECIAL INSTRUCTIONS
Mixes well with lilies, gerbera
daisies, snapdragons, and stock in
country-garden arrangements

DENDROBIUM ORCHID

DOCK

BOTANICAL NAME
Dendrobium nobile; Orchidaceae

SEASON
January through April, September
through December

COLORS
Many colors

SPECIAL INSTRUCTIONS
Very showy blossoms; long sprays
create sweeping lines in
arrangements

BOTANICAL NAME
Rumex crispus; Polygonaceae

SEASON
June through September

COLORS
Red, yellow, brown

SPECIAL INSTRUCTIONS
Dries well

FEVERFEW

BOTANICAL NAME
Chrysanthemum parthenium;
Compositae

SEASON
All year

COLORS
White

SPECIAL INSTRUCTIONS
A very fragrant flower; single and
double blossoms available

FORSYTHIA

BOTANICAL NAME
Forsythia X *intermedia;* Oleaceae

SEASON
All year

COLORS
Yellow

SPECIAL INSTRUCTIONS
Spike flower; dramatic alone in early
spring; mixes well with
spring-blooming flowers such as
irises, tulips, and narcissus

LACE TRUMPET

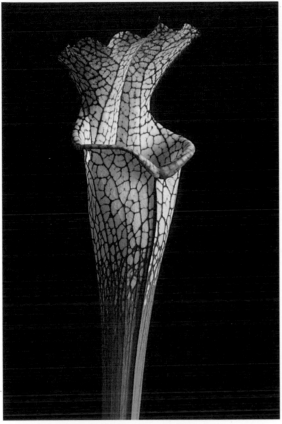

BOTANICAL NAME
Saururs cernuus; Saururaceae

SEASON
June through September

COLORS
White

LIATRIS
or
BLAZING STAR

BOTANICAL NAME
Liatris spicata; Compositae

SEASON
June through December

COLORS
Lavender

SPECIAL INSTRUCTIONS
Good extender in mass
arrangements

LILAC

BOTANICAL NAME
Syringa vulgaris; Oleaceae

SEASON
January through May, November
through December

COLORS
White, lavender, purple, blue

SPECIAL INSTRUCTIONS
Has a woody stem; use stronger
preconditioning solution, available
from your florist

LILY

BOTANICAL NAME
Lilium; Liliaceae

SEASON
All year

COLORS
Yellow, white, orange

SPECIAL INSTRUCTIONS
Purchase in bud stage for a
longer-lasting flower

LILY OF THE VALLEY

BOTANICAL NAME
Convallaria majalis; Liliaceae

SEASON
All year

COLORS
White

SPECIAL INSTRUCTIONS
A very fragrant flower; spike form

MARGUERITE DAISY

BOTANICAL NAME
Anthemis tinctoria; Compositae

SEASON
All year

COLORS
White, yellow

SPECIAL INSTRUCTIONS
Remove foliage before arranging;
good filler for mass arrangements

MARIGOLD

BOTANICAL NAME
Calendula officinalis; Compositae

SEASON
June through mid-September.

COLORS
Many colors

SPECIAL INSTRUCTIONS
A very distinctively fragrant flower,
not sweet, but sharp

MONKSHOOD

BOTANICAL NAME
Aconitum X arendsii;
Ranunculaceae

SEASON
Mid-May through mid-October

COLORS
Purple

SPECIAL INSTRUCTIONS
A good vertical line flower

NARCISSUS
or
DAFFODIL

NERINE LILY

BOTANICAL NAME
Narcissus poeticus; Amaryllidaceae

SEASON
Mid-February through May

COLORS
Yellow and white

SPECIAL INSTRUCTIONS
A very fragrant flower; mixes well
with other spring flowers such as
tulips, irises, and snapdragons

BOTANICAL NAME
Nerine sarniensis; Amaryllidaceae

SEASON
January through March, June
through December

COLORS
Many colors

SPECIAL INSTRUCTIONS
A long-lasting flower

PEONY

BOTANICAL NAME
Paeonia lactiflora; Paeoniaceae

SEASON
May through June

COLORS
Many colors

SPECIAL INSTRUCTIONS
A very fragrant flower; large form
flower

PHLOX

BOTANICAL NAME
Phlox paniculata hybriden;
Polemoniaceae

SEASON
June through September

COLORS
White and lavender

SPECIAL INSTRUCTIONS
A very showy flower; contrasts well
with snapdragons, irises, and tulips

PROTEA

BOTANICAL NAME
Protea; Proteaceae

SEASON
All year

COLORS
Many colors

SPECIAL INSTRUCTIONS
A very long-lasting flower; a dramatic
flower that will add texture

RAMBLING ROSE

BOTANICAL NAME
Rosa multiflora; Rosaceae

SEASON
January through June

COLORS
Many colors

SPECIAL INSTRUCTIONS
Used in mass arrangements; mixes
well with irises, pompom
chrysanthemums, delphinium,
and stock

ROSE
(standard)

BOTANICAL NAME
Rosa hybriden; Rosaceae

SEASON
All year

COLORS
Many colors

SPECIAL INSTRUCTIONS
Be sure to cut stem under water to
prolong life of flower

RUSCUS GREENS

BOTANICAL NAME
Ruscus aculeatus; Liliaceae

SEASON
All year

COLORS
Green foliage

SPECIAL INSTRUCTIONS
Branches may be bleached; leaves
and stems are very ornamental

SCABIOSA

BOTANICAL NAME
Scabiosa caucasica; Dipsacaceae

SEASON
May through mid-October

COLORS
Blue

SPECIAL INSTRUCTIONS
A delicate flower; mixes well with irises, rubrum lilies, Shasta daisies, rambling roses, delphinium, and roses

STAR OF BETHLEHEM

BOTANICAL NAME
Ornithogalum umbellatum; Liliaceae

SEASON
May through December

COLORS
White

SPECIAL INSTRUCTIONS
Plant is poisonous; a long-lasting flower; mixes well with amaryllis, gerbera daisies, freesia, stock, and baby's breath

STATICE

BOTANICAL NAME
Statice sinuata; Plumbaginaceae

SEASON
March through November

COLORS
White, purple, yellow, lavender, pink

SPECIAL INSTRUCTIONS
Dries well; holds its color

STOCK

BOTANICAL NAME
Matthiola incana; Cruciferae

SEASON
April through August

COLORS
Many colors

SPECIAL INSTRUCTIONS
Both single and double flowers; cut
into soft tissue, or split stem 3″;
a very fragrant flower

SWEET PEA

BOTANICAL NAME
Lathyrus odoratus; Leguminosae

SEASON
March through August

COLORS
Many colors

SPECIAL INSTRUCTIONS
Very delicate; mixes well with
brodiaea, miniature roses, and
violets; effective alone; a very
fragrant flower

TUBEROSE

BOTANICAL NAME
Polianthes tuberosa; Agavaceae

SEASON
July through October

COLORS
White

SPECIAL INSTRUCTIONS
Waxy flowers with a very sweet odor

TULIP

ZINNIA

BOTANICAL NAME
Tulipa gesneriana; Liliaceae

SEASON
April through June

COLORS
Many colors

SPECIAL INSTRUCTIONS
Not a long-lasting flower; mixes well
with other spring flowers, such as
irises, hyacinths, narcissus,
and lilies

BOTANICAL NAME
Zinnia elegans; Compositae

SEASON
Mid-July through September

COLORS
Many colors

SPECIAL INSTRUCTIONS
Mixes well with chrysanthemums,
irises, marigolds, and statice in
informal country bouquets

APPENDIX 2

Sources

You can purchase most of your flowers and other basic needs at a local florist or garden center. You will also find some of your floral needs, such as containers, at hardware stores, department stores, variety stores, supermarkets, or ceramic shops.
For special needs—or just for fun—write to the following suppliers and request a catalog.

UNITED STATES

FLOWERS

Ball Seed Co.
P.O. Box 335
West Chicago, IL 60185

Delaware Valley Wholesale
Florist
P.O. Box 415
Sewell, NJ 08080

Denver Wholesale Florist Co.
4800 Dahlia St.
P.O. Box 1138
Denver, CO 80201

"Everything for the Grower"
E.C. Geiger
Box 285, Dept. R
Harleysville, PA 19438

H.G. German Seeds
Box 398
Smethport, PA 16749

IBG—Greenhouse
P.O. Box 100
Wheeling, IL 60090

Kennicott Brothers Co.
2660 N. Clybourn Ave.
Chicago, IL 60614

R.W.T. Nursery—tropical
foliage
12539 Acme Dairy Rd.
Boynton Beach, FL 33435

Wayside Gardens
P.O. Box 1
Hodges, SC 26965

CONTAINERS

Milton Adler
501 Madison Ave.
Atlantic City, NJ 08401

Balos—glassware
2720 N. Paulina St.
Chicago, IL 60614

The Blenko Glass Co.
P.O. Box 67
Milton, WV 22541

E.O. Brody
P.O. Box 22180
Cleveland, OH 44122

Davidson-Uphoff, Inc.
P.O. Box 184
Clarendon Hills, IL 60514

Diamond-Line Container Co.
943 El Dorado Dr.
Akron, OH 44319

Franklin China
112 Terwood Rd.
Willow Grove, PA 19090

Hoosier Glass
P.O. Box 756
Kokomo, IN 46901

Vincent Lippe
11 E. 26th Street
New York, NY 10010

Mottahedeh
225 Fifth Ave.
New York, New York 10010

Pioneer Wholesale Co.
3520 W. 130th Street
Cleveland, OH 44111

Riekes-Crisa Corp.
1818 Leavenworth St.
Omaha, NB 68102

Toscany Imports, Ltd.
245 Fifth Ave.
New York, NY 10016

Toyo Trading Co.
13000 Spring St.
Los Angeles, CA 90061

Two's Company, Inc.
33 Bertel Ave.
Mt. Vernon, NY 10550

SILK FLOWERS

Aldik Artificial Flower Co.
7651 Sepulveda Blvd.
Van Nuys, CA 91405

Caffco
P.O. Box 3508
Montgomery, AL 36193

Designer Accents
10614 King William Dr.
Dallas, TX 75220

DRIED MATERIALS

Knud Nielsen Co.
P.O. Box 746
Evergreen, AL 36401

Vans, Inc.
3730 W. 131st St.
Alsip, IL 60658

ACCESSORIES AND OTHER SUPPLIES

Kurt Adler, Inc.—christmas supplies
1107 Broadway
New York, NY 10010

Best Buy Floral Supply
P.O. Box 1982
Cedar Rapids, IO 52406

Design Master Floral Products
P.O. Box 601
Boulder, CO 80306

Fibre-Form Products
329 Town & Country Village
Palo Alto, CA 94301

Floral Masters International
1111 Hawthorne Lane, Bldg. D
P.O. Box 100
Wheeling, IL 60090

Floralife, Inc.
7 Salt Creek Lane
Hinsdale, IL 60521

Florists Products
2242 N. Palmer Drive
Schaumberg, IL 60195

Hanford's, Inc.
Creators and Importers
1021 E. Independence Blvd.
Charlotte, NC 28232

J.M. Trading Corp.
241 Frontage Road, Suite 31
Burr Ridge, IL 60521

Lomey Florist Supplies
301 Suburban Ave.
P.O. Box 7
Deer Park, NY 11729

Lion Ribbon Co.
100 Metro Way
Secaucus, NJ 07094

Schattur Novelty Corp.
901 Broadway
New York, NY 10003

Schusters of Texas, Inc.—decorative foliage
Box 97
Goldthwaite, TX 76844

Union County Florist Supplies, Inc.
87 Grove Ave.
Staten Island, NY 10302

CANADA

FLOWERS

Aubin Garden Centre
6125 St. Jacques
Montreal, PQ H4A 2G5

Baxter's Flower Shop and Sackville Garden Centre
344 Sackville Dr.
Sackville, NS

Central Plants
Florist & Garden Centre
1408 E. 41st St.
Vancouver, BC V5P 1J7

Golden Oak Garden Centre
7376 Blenheim St.
Vancouver, BC V6N 1S3

Jasmin Nursery Ltd.
6305 Henri Bourassa W.
Montreal, PQ H4R 1C7

Lanark Florist Greenhouse & Garden Centre
646 Oakwood Ave.
Toronto, ON M6E 2Y2

Milligan Brothers Ltd.
618 Bedford Highway
Halifax, NS B3M 2L8

Pacific Flowers (1964) Ltd.
3165 Gamma
Victoria, BC

Weall & Cullen Nurseries, Ltd.
784 Sheppard Ave. E.
Willowdale, ON M6M 5B4

Westside Garden Centre
2741 Eglinton Ave. W.
Toronto, ON M6M 5B4

CONTAINERS

Ashley China, Ltd.
50 Bloor St. W.
Toronto, ON M4W 3L8

Blue Mountain Pottery
Mountain Rd.
Collingwood, ON L97 4M2

Canadiana Pottery
260 Sparks Ave.
Willowdale, ON M2H 2S4

Cassidy's Ltd.
2555 Matte Brossard
Montreal, PQ

Fine Decoration Imports
8431 Main St.
Vancouver, BC V5X 3M3

The Glass Store
569 Mount Pleasant Rd.
Toronto, ON M4S 2M5

Staffordshire Potteries (Canada) Ltd.
1093 Meyerside Dr.
Toronto, ON

Superlux Canada, Ltd.
Place Bonaventure
Montreal, PQ

Western Craft Supply
3376 Burns
Victoria, BC V8Z 3P2

SILK FLOWERS

Bufton's Flowers, Ltd.
3 Bentall Centre
Vancouver, BC

Danson Décor
5430 Ferrier
Montreal, PQ

Design Images, Ltd.
4410 Juneau
Burnaby, BC V5C 4C8

Fine Art Flower Co. Ltd.
4000 St. Patrick
Montreal, PQ H4E 1A4

Fine Decoration Imports, Ltd.
843 Main St.
Vancouver, BC V6A 2V5

The Grapevine
388 Eglinton Ave. W.
Toronto, ON M4P 1L8

Meadowsweet Designs
2644 Yonge St.
Toronto, ON M4P 2J5

Plantart Ltee
4765 Charleroi
Montreal, PQ H4E 1A4

Tina Turnino Decorative Accessories
271 Scarlett Rd.
Toronto, On M6N 4L1

Victoria Fine Flowers
1594 Fairfield Rd.
Victoria, BC V8S 1G1

FLORAL DESIGN SCHOOLS

UNITED STATES

America Floral Art Design
539 S. Wabash
Chicago, IL 60605

Benz School of Floral Design
Drawer MM
College Station, TX 77840

Hixson's Floral Design School
14125 Detroit Ave.
Lakewood, OH 44107

Phil Rulloda
School of Floral Design
1915 E. McDowell Ave.
Phoenix, AZ 85006

Shelton School of Floral Design
8406 Wier Dr.
Houston, TX 77017

CANADA

Fleuriste Emotion
1642 Henri Bourassa E.
Montreal, PQ H2C 1H9

Fleuriste Je T'Aime
5175 Belanger E.
Montreal, PQ H1T 1E1

Fleurs De Venise
7084 St. Laurent
Montreal, PQ H2S 3E2

Lecomte Flowers Ltd.
Toronto Dominion Centre
Toronto, ON

Montreal Floral Art School
5475 Victoria Ave.
Montreal, PQ H3W 2P7

Toronto School of Floral Design
2628 Yonge St.
Toronto, ON M4P 2J4

ENGLAND

Rona Coleman, NDSF
The Old School House
Payford, Redmarley
Gloucestershire
GL19 3HY
England

Fleur De Lys Floral School
2 Royal Ave.
Waltham Cross, Hertsfordshire
EN8 7QS England

Studio of Floristry, London
45 Lansdowne Rd.
Holland Park, London W11
England

Index